The Tragedie of
Romeo and Juliet

By Edward de Vere

Art:
Portrait of Edward de Vere
17th Earl of Oxford (1550-1604)

This edition produced by
Verus Publishing

V | P

www.verusbooks.com

ISBN: 978-1-951267-32-2
Imprint / Publisher: Verus Publishing

The Author

Edward de Vere, 17th Earl of Oxford

Biography and Bibliography
After the Play

A Preverse

Drone on ye learned scholars of the day
As to with whom the words ahead the credit lay.
For our part though can be no further doubt
That the author of these words has been found out
To be a person lordly and refined
On whom the light of wit so boldly shined
That to keep this wit from tearing in the fray
He gave another, lesser wit his say.

Now let the least of wits
That writes these paltry lines
Yield to him whose peerless name
Should be with reverence spake.
Let this name be not of history's misassigns
Whose pen and verse have made the earth to shake.

The Tragedie of
Romeo and Juliet

By Edward de Vere

The Main Characters

In the Ruling house of Verona

Prince Escalus - Prince of Verona.

Count Paris - Kinsman of Escalus, suitor to Juliet

Mercutio - Kinsman of Escalus, a friend of Romeo.

The House of Capulet

Capulet - Patriarch of the house of Capulet.

Lady Capulet - Matriarch of the house of Capulet.

Juliet Capulet - Daughter of Capulet

Tybalt - Cousin of Juliet

Nurse - Juliet's personal attendant and confidante.

Rosaline - Lord Capulet's niece

Peter, Sampson, and Gregory - Servants

The House of Montague

Montague - Patriarch of the house of Montague.

Lady Montague - Matriarch of the house of Montague.

Romeo Montague - The son of Montague

Benvolio - Romeo's cousin and best friend.

Abraham and Balthasar – Servants

Also:

Friar Laurence - Franciscan friar and Romeo's confidant.

And now, the Play…

ACT I
PROLOGUE

Two households, both alike in dignity,
In fair Verona, where we lay our scene,
From ancient grudge break to new mutiny,
Where civil blood makes civil hands unclean.
From forth the fatal loins of these two foes
A pair of star-cross'd lovers take their life;
Whose misadventured piteous overthrows
Do with their death bury their parents' strife.
The fearful passage of their death-mark'd love,
And the continuance of their parents' rage,
Which, but their children's end, nought could remove,
Is now the two hours' traffic of our stage;
The which if you with patient ears attend,
What here shall miss, our toil shall strive to mend.

SCENE I.

Verona. A public place.

*Enter SAMPSON and GREGORY, of the house of Capulet,
armed with swords and bucklers*

SAMPSON
   Gregory, o' my word, we'll not carry coals.
GREGORY
   No, for then we should be colliers.
SAMPSON
   I mean, an we be in choler, we'll draw.
GREGORY
   Ay, while you live, draw your neck out o' the collar.
SAMPSON
   I strike quickly, being moved.

GREGORY
But thou art not quickly moved to strike.
SAMPSON
A dog of the house of Montague moves me.
GREGORY
To move is to stir; and to be valiant is to stand:
therefore, if thou art moved, thou runn'st away.
SAMPSON
A dog of that house shall move me to stand: I will
take the wall of any man or maid of Montague's.
GREGORY
That shows thee a weak slave; for the weakest goes
to the wall.
SAMPSON
True; and therefore women, being the weaker vessels,
are ever thrust to the wall: therefore I will push
Montague's men from the wall, and thrust his maids
to the wall.
GREGORY
The quarrel is between our masters and us their men.
SAMPSON
'Tis all one, I will show myself a tyrant: when I
have fought with the men, I will be cruel with the
maids, and cut off their heads.
GREGORY
The heads of the maids?
SAMPSON
Ay, the heads of the maids, or their maidenheads;
take it in what sense thou wilt.
GREGORY
They must take it in sense that feel it.
SAMPSON
Me they shall feel while I am able to stand: and
'tis known I am a pretty piece of flesh.

GREGORY
'Tis well thou art not fish; if thou hadst, thou
hadst been poor John. Draw thy tool! here comes
two of the house of the Montagues.
SAMPSON
My naked weapon is out: quarrel, I will back thee.
GREGORY
How! turn thy back and run?
SAMPSON
Fear me not.
GREGORY
No, marry; I fear thee!
SAMPSON
Let us take the law of our sides; let them begin.
GREGORY
I will frown as I pass by, and let them take it as
they list.
SAMPSON
Nay, as they dare. I will bite my thumb at them;
which is a disgrace to them, if they bear it.

Enter ABRAHAM and BALTHASAR

ABRAHAM
Do you bite your thumb at us, sir?
SAMPSON
I do bite my thumb, sir.
ABRAHAM
Do you bite your thumb at us, sir?
SAMPSON
[Aside to GREGORY] Is the law of our side, if I say
ay?
GREGORY
No.
SAMPSON

No, sir, I do not bite my thumb at you, sir, but I
bite my thumb, sir.

GREGORY

Do you quarrel, sir?

ABRAHAM

Quarrel sir! no, sir.

SAMPSON

If you do, sir, I am for you: I serve as good a man as
you.

ABRAHAM

No better.

SAMPSON

Well, sir.

GREGORY

Say 'better:' here comes one of my master's kinsmen.

SAMPSON

Yes, better, sir.

ABRAHAM

You lie.

SAMPSON

Draw, if you be men. Gregory, remember thy swashing
blow.

They fight

Enter BENVOLIO

BENVOLIO

Part, fools!
Put up your swords; you know not what you do.
Beats down their swords

Enter TYBALT

TYBALT

What, art thou drawn among these heartless hinds?
Turn thee, Benvolio, look upon thy death.

BENVOLIO

I do but keep the peace: put up thy sword,
Or manage it to part these men with me.

TYBALT

What, drawn, and talk of peace! I hate the word,
As I hate hell, all Montagues, and thee:
Have at thee, coward!

They fight

*Enter, several of both houses, who join the fray; then enter
Citizens, with clubs*

First Citizen

Clubs, bills, and partisans! strike! beat them down!
Down with the Capulets! down with the Montagues!

Enter CAPULET in his gown, and LADY CAPULET

CAPULET

What noise is this? Give me my long sword, ho!

LADY CAPULET

A crutch, a crutch! why call you for a sword?

CAPULET

My sword, I say! Old Montague is come,
And flourishes his blade in spite of me.

Enter MONTAGUE and LADY MONTAGUE

MONTAGUE

Thou villain Capulet,--Hold me not, let me go.

LADY MONTAGUE

Thou shalt not stir a foot to seek a foe.

Romeo and Juliet — Act I

PRINCE
Rebellious subjects, enemies to peace,
Profaners of this neighbour-stained steel,--
Will they not hear? What, ho! you men, you beasts,
That quench the fire of your pernicious rage
With purple fountains issuing from your veins,
On pain of torture, from those bloody hands
Throw your mistemper'd weapons to the ground,
And hear the sentence of your moved prince.
Three civil brawls, bred of an airy word,
By thee, old Capulet, and Montague,
Have thrice disturb'd the quiet of our streets,
And made Verona's ancient citizens
Cast by their grave beseeming ornaments,
To wield old partisans, in hands as old,
Canker'd with peace, to part your canker'd hate:
If ever you disturb our streets again,
Your lives shall pay the forfeit of the peace.
For this time, all the rest depart away:
You Capulet; shall go along with me:
And, Montague, come you this afternoon,
To know our further pleasure in this case,
To old Free-town, our common judgment-place.
Once more, on pain of death, all men depart.

*Exeunt all but MONTAGUE, LADY MONTAGUE, and
BENVOLIO*

MONTAGUE
Who set this ancient quarrel new abroach?
Speak, nephew, were you by when it began?
BENVOLIO
Here were the servants of your adversary,

11

And yours, close fighting ere I did approach:
I drew to part them: in the instant came
The fiery Tybalt, with his sword prepared,
Which, as he breathed defiance to my ears,
He swung about his head and cut the winds,
Who nothing hurt withal hiss'd him in scorn:
While we were interchanging thrusts and blows,
Came more and more and fought on part and part,
Till the prince came, who parted either part.

LADY MONTAGUE
O, where is Romeo? saw you him to-day?
Right glad I am he was not at this fray.

BENVOLIO
Madam, an hour before the worshipp'd sun
Peer'd forth the golden window of the east,
A troubled mind drave me to walk abroad;
Where, underneath the grove of sycamore
That westward rooteth from the city's side,
So early walking did I see your son:
Towards him I made, but he was ware of me
And stole into the covert of the wood:
I, measuring his affections by my own,
That most are busied when they're most alone,
Pursued my humour not pursuing his,
And gladly shunn'd who gladly fled from me.

MONTAGUE
Many a morning hath he there been seen,
With tears augmenting the fresh morning dew.
Adding to clouds more clouds with his deep sighs;
But all so soon as the all-cheering sun
Should in the furthest east begin to draw
The shady curtains from Aurora's bed,
Away from the light steals home my heavy son,
And private in his chamber pens himself,

Shuts up his windows, locks far daylight out
And makes himself an artificial night:
Black and portentous must this humour prove,
Unless good counsel may the cause remove.
BENVOLIO
My noble uncle, do you know the cause?
MONTAGUE
I neither know it nor can learn of him.
BENVOLIO
Have you importuned him by any means?
MONTAGUE
Both by myself and many other friends:
But he, his own affections' counsellor,
Is to himself--I will not say how true--
But to himself so secret and so close,
So far from sounding and discovery,
As is the bud bit with an envious worm,
Ere he can spread his sweet leaves to the air,
Or dedicate his beauty to the sun.
Could we but learn from whence his sorrows grow.
We would as willingly give cure as know.

Enter ROMEO

BENVOLIO
See, where he comes: so please you, step aside;
I'll know his grievance, or be much denied.
MONTAGUE
I would thou wert so happy by thy stay,
To hear true shrift. Come, madam, let's away.

Exeunt MONTAGUE and LADY MONTAGUE

BENVOLIO
Good-morrow, cousin.

ROMEO
  Is the day so young?
BENVOLIO
  But new struck nine.
ROMEO
  Ay me! sad hours seem long.
  Was that my father that went hence so fast?
BENVOLIO
  It was. What sadness lengthens Romeo's hours?
ROMEO
  Not having that, which, having, makes them short.
BENVOLIO
  In love?
ROMEO
  Out--
BENVOLIO
  Of love?
ROMEO
  Out of her favour, where I am in love.
BENVOLIO
  Alas, that love, so gentle in his view,
  Should be so tyrannous and rough in proof!
ROMEO
  Alas, that love, whose view is muffled still,
  Should, without eyes, see pathways to his will!
  Where shall we dine? O me! What fray was here?
  Yet tell me not, for I have heard it all.
  Here's much to do with hate, but more with love.
  Why, then, O brawling love! O loving hate!
  O any thing, of nothing first create!
  O heavy lightness! serious vanity!
  Mis-shapen chaos of well-seeming forms!
  Feather of lead, bright smoke, cold fire,
  sick health!

Still-waking sleep, that is not what it is!
This love feel I, that feel no love in this.
Dost thou not laugh?
BENVOLIO
No, coz, I rather weep.
ROMEO
Good heart, at what?
BENVOLIO
At thy good heart's oppression.
ROMEO
Why, such is love's transgression.
Griefs of mine own lie heavy in my breast,
Which thou wilt propagate, to have it prest
With more of thine: this love that thou hast shown
Doth add more grief to too much of mine own.
Love is a smoke raised with the fume of sighs;
Being purged, a fire sparkling in lovers' eyes;
Being vex'd a sea nourish'd with lovers' tears:
What is it else? a madness most discreet,
A choking gall and a preserving sweet.
Farewell, my coz.
BENVOLIO
Soft! I will go along;
An if you leave me so, you do me wrong.
ROMEO
Tut, I have lost myself; I am not here;
This is not Romeo, he's some other where.
BENVOLIO
Tell me in sadness, who is that you love.
ROMEO
What, shall I groan and tell thee?
BENVOLIO
Groan! why, no.
But sadly tell me who.

ROMEO
Bid a sick man in sadness make his will:
Ah, word ill urged to one that is so ill!
In sadness, cousin, I do love a woman.
BENVOLIO
I aim'd so near, when I supposed you loved.
ROMEO
A right good mark-man! And she's fair I love.
BENVOLIO
A right fair mark, fair coz, is soonest hit.
ROMEO
Well, in that hit you miss: she'll not be hit
With Cupid's arrow; she hath Dian's wit;
And, in strong proof of chastity well arm'd,
From love's weak childish bow she lives unharm'd.
She will not stay the siege of loving terms,
Nor bide the encounter of assailing eyes,
Nor ope her lap to saint-seducing gold:
O, she is rich in beauty, only poor,
That when she dies with beauty dies her store.
BENVOLIO
Then she hath sworn that she will still live chaste?
ROMEO
She hath, and in that sparing makes huge waste,
For beauty starved with her severity
Cuts beauty off from all posterity.
She is too fair, too wise, wisely too fair,
To merit bliss by making me despair:
She hath forsworn to love, and in that vow
Do I live dead that live to tell it now.
BENVOLIO
Be ruled by me, forget to think of her.
ROMEO
O, teach me how I should forget to think.

BENVOLIO
By giving liberty unto thine eyes;
Examine other beauties.

ROMEO
'Tis the way
To call hers exquisite, in question more:
These happy masks that kiss fair ladies' brows
Being black put us in mind they hide the fair;
He that is strucken blind cannot forget
The precious treasure of his eyesight lost:
Show me a mistress that is passing fair,
What doth her beauty serve, but as a note
Where I may read who pass'd that passing fair?
Farewell: thou canst not teach me to forget.

BENVOLIO
I'll pay that doctrine, or else die in debt.

Exeunt

SCENE II.

A street.

Enter CAPULET, PARIS, and Servant

CAPULET
But Montague is bound as well as I,
In penalty alike; and 'tis not hard, I think,
For men so old as we to keep the peace.

PARIS
Of honourable reckoning are you both;
And pity 'tis you lived at odds so long.
But now, my lord, what say you to my suit?

CAPULET
But saying o'er what I have said before:
My child is yet a stranger in the world;

She hath not seen the change of fourteen years,
Let two more summers wither in their pride,
Ere we may think her ripe to be a bride.
PARIS
Younger than she are happy mothers made.
CAPULET
And too soon marr'd are those so early made.
The earth hath swallow'd all my hopes but she,
She is the hopeful lady of my earth:
But woo her, gentle Paris, get her heart,
My will to her consent is but a part;
An she agree, within her scope of choice
Lies my consent and fair according voice.
This night I hold an old accustom'd feast,
Whereto I have invited many a guest,
Such as I love; and you, among the store,
One more, most welcome, makes my number more.
At my poor house look to behold this night
Earth-treading stars that make dark heaven light:
Such comfort as do lusty young men feel
When well-apparell'd April on the heel
Of limping winter treads, even such delight
Among fresh female buds shall you this night
Inherit at my house; hear all, all see,
And like her most whose merit most shall be:
Which on more view, of many mine being one
May stand in number, though in reckoning none,
Come, go with me.

To Servant, giving a paper

Go, sirrah, trudge about
Through fair Verona; find those persons out
Whose names are written there, and to them say,
My house and welcome on their pleasure stay.

Romeo and Juliet — Act I

Exeunt CAPULET and PARIS

Servant
Find them out whose names are written here! It is
written, that the shoemaker should meddle with his
yard, and the tailor with his last, the fisher with
his pencil, and the painter with his nets; but I am
sent to find those persons whose names are here
writ, and can never find what names the writing
person hath here writ. I must to the learned.--In good
time.

Enter BENVOLIO and ROMEO

BENVOLIO
Tut, man, one fire burns out another's burning,
One pain is lessen'd by another's anguish;
Turn giddy, and be holp by backward turning;
One desperate grief cures with another's languish:
Take thou some new infection to thy eye,
And the rank poison of the old will die.
ROMEO
Your plaintain-leaf is excellent for that.
BENVOLIO
For what, I pray thee?
ROMEO
For your broken shin.
BENVOLIO
Why, Romeo, art thou mad?
ROMEO
Not mad, but bound more than a mad-man is;
Shut up in prison, kept without my food,
Whipp'd and tormented and--God-den, good fellow.
Servant
God gi' god-den. I pray, sir, can you read?

19

ROMEO
 Ay, mine own fortune in my misery.
Servant
 Perhaps you have learned it without book: but, I
 pray, can you read any thing you see?
ROMEO
 Ay, if I know the letters and the language.
Servant
 Ye say honestly: rest you merry!
ROMEO
 Stay, fellow; I can read.

Reads

'Signior Martino and his wife and daughters;
County Anselme and his beauteous sisters; the lady
widow of Vitravio; Signior Placentio and his lovely
nieces; Mercutio and his brother Valentine; mine
uncle Capulet, his wife and daughters; my fair niece
Rosaline; Livia; Signior Valentio and his cousin
Tybalt, Lucio and the lively Helena.' A fair
assembly: whither should they come?
Servant
 Up.
ROMEO
 Whither?
Servant
 To supper; to our house.
ROMEO
 Whose house?
Servant
 My master's.
ROMEO
 Indeed, I should have ask'd you that before.
Servant

Now I'll tell you without asking: my master is the
great rich Capulet; and if you be not of the house
of Montagues, I pray, come and crush a cup of wine.
Rest you merry!

Exit

BENVOLIO
At this same ancient feast of Capulet's
Sups the fair Rosaline whom thou so lovest,
With all the admired beauties of Verona:
Go thither; and, with unattainted eye,
Compare her face with some that I shall show,
And I will make thee think thy swan a crow.
ROMEO
When the devout religion of mine eye
Maintains such falsehood, then turn tears to fires;
And these, who often drown'd could never die,
Transparent heretics, be burnt for liars!
One fairer than my love! the all-seeing sun
Ne'er saw her match since first the world begun.
BENVOLIO
Tut, you saw her fair, none else being by,
Herself poised with herself in either eye:
But in that crystal scales let there be weigh'd
Your lady's love against some other maid
That I will show you shining at this feast,
And she shall scant show well that now shows best.
ROMEO
I'll go along, no such sight to be shown,
But to rejoice in splendor of mine own.

Exeunt

SCENE III.

A room in Capulet's house.

Enter LADY CAPULET and Nurse

LADY CAPULET
  Nurse, where's my daughter? call her forth to me.
Nurse
  Now, by my maidenhead, at twelve year old,
  I bade her come. What, lamb! what, ladybird!
  God forbid! Where's this girl? What, Juliet!

Enter JULIET

JULIET
  How now! who calls?
Nurse
  Your mother.
JULIET
  Madam, I am here.
  What is your will?
LADY CAPULET
  This is the matter:--Nurse, give leave awhile,
  We must talk in secret:--nurse, come back again;
  I have remember'd me, thou's hear our counsel.
  Thou know'st my daughter's of a pretty age.
Nurse
  Faith, I can tell her age unto an hour.
LADY CAPULET
  She's not fourteen.
Nurse
  I'll lay fourteen of my teeth,--
  And yet, to my teeth be it spoken, I have but four--
  She is not fourteen. How long is it now
  To Lammas-tide?
LADY CAPULET

A fortnight and odd days.

Nurse

Even or odd, of all days in the year,
Come Lammas-eve at night shall she be fourteen.
Susan and she--God rest all Christian souls!--
Were of an age: well, Susan is with God;
She was too good for me: but, as I said,
On Lammas-eve at night shall she be fourteen;
That shall she, marry; I remember it well.
'Tis since the earthquake now eleven years;
And she was wean'd,--I never shall forget it,--
Of all the days of the year, upon that day:
For I had then laid wormwood to my dug,
Sitting in the sun under the dove-house wall;
My lord and you were then at Mantua:--
Nay, I do bear a brain:--but, as I said,
When it did taste the wormwood on the nipple
Of my dug and felt it bitter, pretty fool,
To see it tetchy and fall out with the dug!
Shake quoth the dove-house: 'twas no need, I trow,
To bid me trudge:
And since that time it is eleven years;
For then she could stand alone; nay, by the rood,
She could have run and waddled all about;
For even the day before, she broke her brow:
And then my husband--God be with his soul!
A' was a merry man--took up the child:
'Yea,' quoth he, 'dost thou fall upon thy face?
Thou wilt fall backward when thou hast more wit;
Wilt thou not, Jule?' and, by my holidame,
The pretty wretch left crying and said 'Ay.'
To see, now, how a jest shall come about!
I warrant, an I should live a thousand years,
I never should forget it: 'Wilt thou not, Jule?' quoth he;

And, pretty fool, it stinted and said 'Ay.'
LADY CAPULET
Enough of this; I pray thee, hold thy peace.
Nurse
Yes, madam: yet I cannot choose but laugh,
To think it should leave crying and say 'Ay.'
And yet, I warrant, it had upon its brow
A bump as big as a young cockerel's stone;
A parlous knock; and it cried bitterly:
'Yea,' quoth my husband,'fall'st upon thy face?
Thou wilt fall backward when thou comest to age;
Wilt thou not, Jule?' it stinted and said 'Ay.'
JULIET
And stint thou too, I pray thee, nurse, say I.
Nurse
Peace, I have done. God mark thee to his grace!
Thou wast the prettiest babe that e'er I nursed:
An I might live to see thee married once,
I have my wish.
LADY CAPULET
Marry, that 'marry' is the very theme
I came to talk of. Tell me, daughter Juliet,
How stands your disposition to be married?
JULIET
It is an honour that I dream not of.
Nurse
An honour! were not I thine only nurse,
I would say thou hadst suck'd wisdom from thy teat.
LADY CAPULET
Well, think of marriage now; younger than you,
Here in Verona, ladies of esteem,
Are made already mothers: by my count,
I was your mother much upon these years
That you are now a maid. Thus then in brief:

The valiant Paris seeks you for his love.
Nurse
    A man, young lady! lady, such a man
    As all the world--why, he's a man of wax.
LADY CAPULET
    Verona's summer hath not such a flower.
Nurse
    Nay, he's a flower; in faith, a very flower.
LADY CAPULET
    What say you? can you love the gentleman?
    This night you shall behold him at our feast;
    Read o'er the volume of young Paris' face,
    And find delight writ there with beauty's pen;
    Examine every married lineament,
    And see how one another lends content
    And what obscured in this fair volume lies
    Find written in the margent of his eyes.
    This precious book of love, this unbound lover,
    To beautify him, only lacks a cover:
    The fish lives in the sea, and 'tis much pride
    For fair without the fair within to hide:
    That book in many's eyes doth share the glory,
    That in gold clasps locks in the golden story;
    So shall you share all that he doth possess,
    By having him, making yourself no less.
Nurse
    No less! nay, bigger; women grow by men.
LADY CAPULET
    Speak briefly, can you like of Paris' love?
JULIET
    I'll look to like, if looking liking move:
    But no more deep will I endart mine eye
    Than your consent gives strength to make it fly.

Enter a Servant

Servant
  Madam, the guests are come, supper served up, you
  called, my young lady asked for, the nurse cursed in
  the pantry, and every thing in extremity. I must
  hence to wait; I beseech you, follow straight.
LADY CAPULET
  We follow thee.

Exit Servant

  Juliet, the county stays.
Nurse
  Go, girl, seek happy nights to happy days.

Exeunt

SCENE IV.
A street.

*Enter ROMEO, MERCUTIO, BENVOLIO, with five or six
Maskers, Torch-bearers, and others*

ROMEO
  What, shall this speech be spoke for our excuse?
  Or shall we on without a apology?
BENVOLIO
  The date is out of such prolixity:
  We'll have no Cupid hoodwink'd with a scarf,
  Bearing a Tartar's painted bow of lath,
  Scaring the ladies like a crow-keeper;
  Nor no without-book prologue, faintly spoke
  After the prompter, for our entrance:
  But let them measure us by what they will;
  We'll measure them a measure, and be gone.
ROMEO

Give me a torch: I am not for this ambling;
Being but heavy, I will bear the light.
MERCUTIO
Nay, gentle Romeo, we must have you dance.
ROMEO
Not I, believe me: you have dancing shoes
With nimble soles: I have a soul of lead
So stakes me to the ground I cannot move.
MERCUTIO
You are a lover; borrow Cupid's wings,
And soar with them above a common bound.
ROMEO
I am too sore enpierced with his shaft
To soar with his light feathers, and so bound,
I cannot bound a pitch above dull woe:
Under love's heavy burden do I sink.
MERCUTIO
And, to sink in it, should you burden love;
Too great oppression for a tender thing.
ROMEO
Is love a tender thing? it is too rough,
Too rude, too boisterous, and it pricks like thorn.
MERCUTIO
If love be rough with you, be rough with love;
Prick love for pricking, and you beat love down.
Give me a case to put my visage in:
A visor for a visor! what care I
What curious eye doth quote deformities?
Here are the beetle brows shall blush for me.
BENVOLIO
Come, knock and enter; and no sooner in,
But every man betake him to his legs.
ROMEO
A torch for me: let wantons light of heart

Tickle the senseless rushes with their heels,
For I am proverb'd with a grandsire phrase;
I'll be a candle-holder, and look on.
The game was ne'er so fair, and I am done.
MERCUTIO
Tut, dun's the mouse, the constable's own word:
If thou art dun, we'll draw thee from the mire
Of this sir-reverence love, wherein thou stick'st
Up to the ears. Come, we burn daylight, ho!
ROMEO
Nay, that's not so.
MERCUTIO
I mean, sir, in delay
We waste our lights in vain, like lamps by day.
Take our good meaning, for our judgment sits
Five times in that ere once in our five wits.
ROMEO
And we mean well in going to this mask;
But 'tis no wit to go.
MERCUTIO
Why, may one ask?
ROMEO
I dream'd a dream to-night.
MERCUTIO
And so did I.
ROMEO
Well, what was yours?
MERCUTIO
That dreamers often lie.
ROMEO
In bed asleep, while they do dream things true.
MERCUTIO
O, then, I see Queen Mab hath been with you.
She is the fairies' midwife, and she comes

In shape no bigger than an agate-stone
On the fore-finger of an alderman,
Drawn with a team of little atomies
Athwart men's noses as they lie asleep;
Her wagon-spokes made of long spiders' legs,
The cover of the wings of grasshoppers,
The traces of the smallest spider's web,
The collars of the moonshine's watery beams,
Her whip of cricket's bone, the lash of film,
Her wagoner a small grey-coated gnat,
Not so big as a round little worm
Prick'd from the lazy finger of a maid;
Her chariot is an empty hazel-nut
Made by the joiner squirrel or old grub,
Time out o' mind the fairies' coachmakers.
And in this state she gallops night by night
Through lovers' brains, and then they dream of love;
O'er courtiers' knees, that dream on court'sies straight,
O'er lawyers' fingers, who straight dream on fees,
O'er ladies ' lips, who straight on kisses dream,
Which oft the angry Mab with blisters plagues,
Because their breaths with sweetmeats tainted are:
Sometime she gallops o'er a courtier's nose,
And then dreams he of smelling out a suit;
And sometime comes she with a tithe-pig's tail
Tickling a parson's nose as a' lies asleep,
Then dreams, he of another benefice:
Sometime she driveth o'er a soldier's neck,
And then dreams he of cutting foreign throats,
Of breaches, ambuscadoes, Spanish blades,
Of healths five-fathom deep; and then anon
Drums in his ear, at which he starts and wakes,
And being thus frighted swears a prayer or two
And sleeps again. This is that very Mab

That plats the manes of horses in the night,
And bakes the elflocks in foul sluttish hairs,
Which once untangled, much misfortune bodes:
This is the hag, when maids lie on their backs,
That presses them and learns them first to bear,
Making them women of good carriage:
This is she--
ROMEO
Peace, peace, Mercutio, peace!
Thou talk'st of nothing.
MERCUTIO
True, I talk of dreams,
Which are the children of an idle brain,
Begot of nothing but vain fantasy,
Which is as thin of substance as the air
And more inconstant than the wind, who wooes
Even now the frozen bosom of the north,
And, being anger'd, puffs away from thence,
Turning his face to the dew-dropping south.
BENVOLIO
This wind, you talk of, blows us from ourselves;
Supper is done, and we shall come too late.
ROMEO
I fear, too early: for my mind misgives
Some consequence yet hanging in the stars
Shall bitterly begin his fearful date
With this night's revels and expire the term
Of a despised life closed in my breast
By some vile forfeit of untimely death.
But He, that hath the steerage of my course,
Direct my sail! On, lusty gentlemen.
BENVOLIO
Strike, drum.

Exeunt

30

SCENE V.

A hall in Capulet's house.

Musicians waiting. Enter Servingmen with napkins

First Servant
Where's Potpan, that he helps not to take away? He
shift a trencher? he scrape a trencher!
Second Servant
When good manners shall lie all in one or two men's
hands and they unwashed too, 'tis a foul thing.
First Servant
Away with the joint-stools, remove the
court-cupboard, look to the plate. Good thou, save
me a piece of marchpane; and, as thou lovest me, let
the porter let in Susan Grindstone and Nell.
Antony, and Potpan!
Second Servant
Ay, boy, ready.
First Servant
You are looked for and called for, asked for and
sought for, in the great chamber.
Second Servant
We cannot be here and there too. Cheerly, boys; be
brisk awhile, and the longer liver take all.

Enter CAPULET, with JULIET and others of his house,
meeting the Guests and Maskers

CAPULET
Welcome, gentlemen! ladies that have their toes
Unplagued with corns will have a bout with you.
Ah ha, my mistresses! which of you all
Will now deny to dance? she that makes dainty,

31

She, I'll swear, hath corns; am I come near ye now?
Welcome, gentlemen! I have seen the day
That I have worn a visor and could tell
A whispering tale in a fair lady's ear,
Such as would please: 'tis gone, 'tis gone, 'tis gone:
You are welcome, gentlemen! come, musicians, play.
A hall, a hall! give room! and foot it, girls.

Music plays, and they dance

More light, you knaves; and turn the tables up,
And quench the fire, the room is grown too hot.
Ah, sirrah, this unlook'd-for sport comes well.
Nay, sit, nay, sit, good cousin Capulet;
For you and I are past our dancing days:
How long is't now since last yourself and I
Were in a mask?
Second Capulet
    By'r lady, thirty years.
CAPULET
    What, man! 'tis not so much, 'tis not so much:
    'Tis since the nuptials of Lucentio,
    Come pentecost as quickly as it will,
    Some five and twenty years; and then we mask'd.
Second Capulet
    'Tis more, 'tis more, his son is elder, sir;
    His son is thirty.
CAPULET
    Will you tell me that?
    His son was but a ward two years ago.
ROMEO
    [To a Servingman] What lady is that, which doth
    enrich the hand
    Of yonder knight?
Servant

I know not, sir.
ROMEO
O, she doth teach the torches to burn bright!
It seems she hangs upon the cheek of night
Like a rich jewel in an Ethiope's ear;
Beauty too rich for use, for earth too dear!
So shows a snowy dove trooping with crows,
As yonder lady o'er her fellows shows.
The measure done, I'll watch her place of stand,
And, touching hers, make blessed my rude hand.
Did my heart love till now? forswear it, sight!
For I ne'er saw true beauty till this night.
TYBALT
This, by his voice, should be a Montague.
Fetch me my rapier, boy. What dares the slave
Come hither, cover'd with an antic face,
To fleer and scorn at our solemnity?
Now, by the stock and honour of my kin,
To strike him dead, I hold it not a sin.
CAPULET
Why, how now, kinsman! wherefore storm you so?
TYBALT
Uncle, this is a Montague, our foe,
A villain that is hither come in spite,
To scorn at our solemnity this night.
CAPULET
Young Romeo is it?
TYBALT
'Tis he, that villain Romeo.
CAPULET
Content thee, gentle coz, let him alone;
He bears him like a portly gentleman;
And, to say truth, Verona brags of him
To be a virtuous and well-govern'd youth:

I would not for the wealth of all the town
Here in my house do him disparagement:
Therefore be patient, take no note of him:
It is my will, the which if thou respect,
Show a fair presence and put off these frowns,
And ill-beseeming semblance for a feast.

TYBALT

It fits, when such a villain is a guest:
I'll not endure him.

CAPULET

He shall be endured:
What, goodman boy! I say, he shall: go to;
Am I the master here, or you? go to.
You'll not endure him! God shall mend my soul!
You'll make a mutiny among my guests!
You will set cock-a-hoop! you'll be the man!

TYBALT

Why, uncle, 'tis a shame.

CAPULET

Go to, go to;
You are a saucy boy: is't so, indeed?
This trick may chance to scathe you, I know what:
You must contrary me! marry, 'tis time.
Well said, my hearts! You are a princox; go:
Be quiet, or--More light, more light! For shame!
I'll make you quiet. What, cheerly, my hearts!

TYBALT

Patience perforce with wilful choler meeting
Makes my flesh tremble in their different greeting.
I will withdraw: but this intrusion shall
Now seeming sweet convert to bitter gall.

Exit

ROMEO

[To JULIET] If I profane with my unworthiest hand
This holy shrine, the gentle fine is this:
My lips, two blushing pilgrims, ready stand
To smooth that rough touch with a tender kiss.
JULIET
Good pilgrim, you do wrong your hand too much,
Which mannerly devotion shows in this;
For saints have hands that pilgrims' hands do touch,
And palm to palm is holy palmers' kiss.
ROMEO
Have not saints lips, and holy palmers too?
JULIET
Ay, pilgrim, lips that they must use in prayer.
ROMEO
O, then, dear saint, let lips do what hands do;
They pray, grant thou, lest faith turn to despair.
JULIET
Saints do not move, though grant for prayers' sake.
ROMEO
Then move not, while my prayer's effect I take.
Thus from my lips, by yours, my sin is purged.
JULIET
Then have my lips the sin that they have took.
ROMEO
Sin from thy lips? O trespass sweetly urged!
Give me my sin again.
JULIET
You kiss by the book.
Nurse
Madam, your mother craves a word with you.
ROMEO
What is her mother?
Nurse
Marry, bachelor,

Her mother is the lady of the house,
And a good lady, and a wise and virtuous
I nursed her daughter, that you talk'd withal;
I tell you, he that can lay hold of her
Shall have the chinks.

ROMEO
Is she a Capulet?
O dear account! my life is my foe's debt.

BENVOLIO
Away, begone; the sport is at the best.

ROMEO
Ay, so I fear; the more is my unrest.

CAPULET
Nay, gentlemen, prepare not to be gone;
We have a trifling foolish banquet towards.
Is it e'en so? why, then, I thank you all
I thank you, honest gentlemen; good night.
More torches here! Come on then, let's to bed.
Ah, sirrah, by my fay, it waxes late:
I'll to my rest.

Exeunt all but JULIET and Nurse

JULIET
Come hither, nurse. What is yond gentleman?

Nurse
The son and heir of old Tiberio.

JULIET
What's he that now is going out of door?

Nurse
Marry, that, I think, be young Petrucio.

JULIET
What's he that follows there, that would not dance?

Nurse
I know not.

Romeo and Juliet — Act I

JULIET
Go ask his name: if he be married.
My grave is like to be my wedding bed.
Nurse
His name is Romeo, and a Montague;
The only son of your great enemy.
JULIET
My only love sprung from my only hate!
Too early seen unknown, and known too late!
Prodigious birth of love it is to me,
That I must love a loathed enemy.
Nurse
What's this? what's this?
JULIET
A rhyme I learn'd even now
Of one I danced withal.

One calls within 'Juliet.'

Nurse
Anon, anon!
Come, let's away; the strangers all are gone.

Exeunt

ACT II
PROLOGUE

Enter Chorus

Chorus
Now old desire doth in his death-bed lie,
And young affection gapes to be his heir;
That fair for which love groan'd for and would die,
With tender Juliet match'd, is now not fair.
Now Romeo is beloved and loves again,
Alike betwitched by the charm of looks,
But to his foe supposed he must complain,
And she steal love's sweet bait from fearful hooks:
Being held a foe, he may not have access
To breathe such vows as lovers use to swear;
And she as much in love, her means much less
To meet her new-beloved any where:
But passion lends them power, time means, to meet
Tempering extremities with extreme sweet.

Exit

SCENE I.
A lane by the wall of Capulet's orchard.

Enter ROMEO

ROMEO
Can I go forward when my heart is here?
Turn back, dull earth, and find thy centre out.

He climbs the wall, and leaps down within it

Romeo and Juliet — Act II

Enter BENVOLIO and MERCUTIO

BENVOLIO
Romeo! my cousin Romeo!
MERCUTIO
He is wise;
And, on my lie, hath stol'n him home to bed.
BENVOLIO
He ran this way, and leap'd this orchard wall:
Call, good Mercutio.
MERCUTIO
Nay, I'll conjure too.
Romeo! humours! madman! passion! lover!
Appear thou in the likeness of a sigh:
Speak but one rhyme, and I am satisfied;
Cry but 'Ay me!' pronounce but 'love' and 'dove;'
Speak to my gossip Venus one fair word,
One nick-name for her purblind son and heir,
Young Adam Cupid, he that shot so trim,
When King Cophetua loved the beggar-maid!
He heareth not, he stirreth not, he moveth not;
The ape is dead, and I must conjure him.
I conjure thee by Rosaline's bright eyes,
By her high forehead and her scarlet lip,
By her fine foot, straight leg and quivering thigh
And the demesnes that there adjacent lie,
That in thy likeness thou appear to us!
BENVOLIO
And if he hear thee, thou wilt anger him.
MERCUTIO
This cannot anger him: 'twould anger him
To raise a spirit in his mistress' circle
Of some strange nature, letting it there stand
Till she had laid it and conjured it down;

That were some spite: my invocation
Is fair and honest, and in his mistres s' name
I conjure only but to raise up him.
BENVOLIO
Come, he hath hid himself among these trees,
To be consorted with the humorous night:
Blind is his love and best befits the dark.
MERCUTIO
If love be blind, love cannot hit the mark.
Now will he sit under a medlar tree,
And wish his mistress were that kind of fruit
As maids call medlars, when they laugh alone.
Romeo, that she were, O, that she were
An open et caetera, thou a poperin pear!
Romeo, good night: I'll to my truckle-bed;
This field-bed is too cold for me to sleep:
Come, shall we go?
BENVOLIO
Go, then; for 'tis in vain
To seek him here that means not to be found.

Exeunt

SCENE II.
Capulet's orchard.

Enter ROMEO

ROMEO
He jests at scars that never felt a wound.

JULIET appears above at a window

But, soft! what light through yonder window breaks?
It is the east, and Juliet is the sun.

Arise, fair sun, and kill the envious moon,
Who is already sick and pale with grief,
That thou her maid art far more fair than she:
Be not her maid, since she is envious;
Her vestal livery is but sick and green
And none but fools do wear it; cast it off.
It is my lady, O, it is my love!
O, that she knew she were!
She speaks yet she says nothing: what of that?
Her eye discourses; I will answer it.
I am too bold, 'tis not to me she speaks:
Two of the fairest stars in all the heaven,
Having some business, do entreat her eyes
To twinkle in their spheres till they return.
What if her eyes were there, they in her head?
The brightness of her cheek would shame those stars,
As daylight doth a lamp; her eyes in heaven
Would through the airy region stream so bright
That birds would sing and think it were not night.
See, how she leans her cheek upon her hand!
O, that I were a glove upon that hand,
That I might touch that cheek!
JULIET
  Ay me!
ROMEO
  She speaks:
  O, speak again, bright angel! for thou art
  As glorious to this night, being o'er my head
  As is a winged messenger of heaven
  Unto the white-upturned wondering eyes
  Of mortals that fall back to gaze on him
  When he bestrides the lazy-pacing clouds
  And sails upon the bosom of the air.
JULIET

O Romeo, Romeo! wherefore art thou Romeo?
Deny thy father and refuse thy name;
Or, if thou wilt not, be but sworn my love,
And I'll no longer be a Capulet.
ROMEO
[Aside] Shall I hear more, or shall I speak at this?
JULIET
'Tis but thy name that is my enemy;
Thou art thyself, though not a Montague.
What's Montague? it is nor hand, nor foot,
Nor arm, nor face, nor any other part
Belonging to a man. O, be some other name!
What's in a name? that which we call a rose
By any other name would smell as sweet;
So Romeo would, were he not Romeo call'd,
Retain that dear perfection which he owes
Without that title. Romeo, doff thy name,
And for that name which is no part of thee
Take all myself.
ROMEO
I take thee at thy word:
Call me but love, and I'll be new baptized;
Henceforth I never will be Romeo.
JULIET
What man art thou that thus bescreen'd in night
So stumblest on my counsel?
ROMEO
By a name
I know not how to tell thee who I am:
My name, dear saint, is hateful to myself,
Because it is an enemy to thee;
Had I it written, I would tear the word.
JULIET
My ears have not yet drunk a hundred words

Of that tongue's utterance, yet I know the sound:
Art thou not Romeo and a Montague?
ROMEO
Neither, fair saint, if either thee dislike.
JULIET
How camest thou hither, tell me, and wherefore?
The orchard walls are high and hard to climb,
And the place death, considering who thou art,
If any of my kinsmen find thee here.
ROMEO
With love's light wings did I o'er-perch these walls;
For stony limits cannot hold love out,
And what love can do that dares love attempt;
Therefore thy kinsmen are no let to me.
JULIET
If they do see thee, they will murder thee.
ROMEO
Alack, there lies more peril in thine eye
Than twenty of their swords: look thou but sweet,
And I am proof against their enmity.
JULIET
I would not for the world they saw thee here.
ROMEO
I have night's cloak to hide me from their sight;
And but thou love me, let them find me here:
My life were better ended by their hate,
Than death prorogued, wanting of thy love.
JULIET
By whose direction found'st thou out this place?
ROMEO
By love, who first did prompt me to inquire;
He lent me counsel and I lent him eyes.
I am no pilot; yet, wert thou as far
As that vast shore wash'd with the farthest sea,

I would adventure for such merchandise.
JULIET
Thou know'st the mask of night is on my face,
Else would a maiden blush bepaint my cheek
For that which thou hast heard me speak to-night
Fain would I dwell on form, fain, fain deny
What I have spoke: but farewell compliment!
Dost thou love me? I know thou wilt say 'Ay,'
And I will take thy word: yet if thou swear'st,
Thou mayst prove false; at lovers' perjuries
Then say, Jove laughs. O gentle Romeo,
If thou dost love, pronounce it faithfully:
Or if thou think'st I am too quickly won,
I'll frown and be perverse an say thee nay,
So thou wilt woo; but else, not for the world.
In truth, fair Montague, I am too fond,
And therefore thou mayst think my 'havior light:
But trust me, gentleman, I'll prove more true
Than those that have more cunning to be strange.
I should have been more strange, I must confess,
But that thou overheard'st, ere I was ware,
My true love's passion: therefore pardon me,
And not impute this yielding to light love,
Which the dark night hath so discovered.
ROMEO
Lady, by yonder blessed moon I swear
That tips with silver all these fruit-tree tops--
JULIET
O, swear not by the moon, the inconstant moon,
That monthly changes in her circled orb,
Lest that thy love prove likewise variable.
ROMEO
What shall I swear by?
JULIET

Do not swear at all;
Or, if thou wilt, swear by thy gracious self,
Which is the god of my idolatry,
And I'll believe thee.
ROMEO
　If my heart's dear love--
JULIET
　Well, do not swear: although I joy in thee,
　I have no joy of this contract to-night:
　It is too rash, too unadvised, too sudden;
　Too like the lightning, which doth cease to be
　Ere one can say 'It lightens.' Sweet, good night!
　This bud of love, by summer's ripening breath,
　May prove a beauteous flower when next we meet.
　Good night, good night! as sweet repose and rest
　Come to thy heart as that within my breast!
ROMEO
　O, wilt thou leave me so unsatisfied?
JULIET
　What satisfaction canst thou have to-night?
ROMEO
　The exchange of thy love's faithful vow for mine.
JULIET
　I gave thee mine before thou didst request it:
　And yet I would it were to give again.
ROMEO
　Wouldst thou withdraw it? for what purpose, love?
JULIET
　But to be frank, and give it thee again.
　And yet I wish but for the thing I have:
　My bounty is as boundless as the sea,
　My love as deep; the more I give to thee,
　The more I have, for both are infinite.

Nurse calls within

45

I hear some noise within; dear love, adieu!
Anon, good nurse! Sweet Montague, be true.
Stay but a little, I will come again.

Exit, above

ROMEO
O blessed, blessed night! I am afeard.
Being in night, all this is but a dream,
Too flattering-sweet to be substantial.

Re-enter JULIET, above

JULIET
Three words, dear Romeo, and good night indeed.
If that thy bent of love be honourable,
Thy purpose marriage, send me word to-morrow,
By one that I'll procure to come to thee,
Where and what time thou wilt perform the rite;
And all my fortunes at thy foot I'll lay
And follow thee my lord throughout the world.
Nurse
[Within] Madam!
JULIET
I come, anon.--But if thou mean'st not well,
I do beseech thee--
Nurse
[Within] Madam!
JULIET
By and by, I come:--
To cease thy suit, and leave me to my grief:
To-morrow will I send.
ROMEO
So thrive my soul--

JULIET
A thousand times good night!

Exit, above

ROMEO
A thousand times the worse, to want thy light.
Love goes toward love, as schoolboys from
their books,
But love from love, toward school with heavy looks.

Retiring

Re-enter JULIET, above

JULIET
Hist! Romeo, hist! O, for a falconer's voice,
To lure this tassel-gentle back again!
Bondage is hoarse, and may not speak aloud;
Else would I tear the cave where Echo lies,
And make her airy tongue more hoarse than mine,
With repetition of my Romeo's name.
ROMEO
It is my soul that calls upon my name:
How silver-sweet sound lovers' tongues by night,
Like softest music to attending ears!
JULIET
Romeo!
ROMEO
My dear?
JULIET
At what o'clock to-morrow
Shall I send to thee?
ROMEO
At the hour of nine.

JULIET
> I will not fail: 'tis twenty years till then.
> I have forgot why I did call thee back.

ROMEO
> Let me stand here till thou remember it.

JULIET
> I shall forget, to have thee still stand there,
> Remembering how I love thy company.

ROMEO
> And I'll still stay, to have thee still forget,
> Forgetting any other home but this.

JULIET
> 'Tis almost morning; I would have thee gone:
> And yet no further than a wanton's bird;
> Who lets it hop a little from her hand,
> Like a poor prisoner in his twisted gyves,
> And with a silk thread plucks it back again,
> So loving-jealous of his liberty.

ROMEO
> I would I were thy bird.

JULIET
> Sweet, so would I:
> Yet I should kill thee with much cherishing.
> Good night, good night! parting is such
> sweet sorrow,
> That I shall say good night till it be morrow.

Exit above

ROMEO
> Sleep dwell upon thine eyes, peace in thy breast!
> Would I were sleep and peace, so sweet to rest!
> Hence will I to my ghostly father's cell,
> His help to crave, and my dear hap to tell.

Exit

SCENE III.

Friar Laurence's cell.

Enter FRIAR LAURENCE, with a basket

FRIAR LAURENCE
   The grey-eyed morn smiles on the frowning night,
   Chequering the eastern clouds with streaks of light,
   And flecked darkness like a drunkard reels
   From forth day's path and Titan's fiery wheels:
   Now, ere the sun advance his burning eye,
   The day to cheer and night's dank dew to dry,
   I must up-fill this osier cage of ours
   With baleful weeds and precious-juiced flowers.
   The earth that's nature's mother is her tomb;
   What is her burying grave that is her womb,
   And from her womb children of divers kind
   We sucking on her natural bosom find,
   Many for many virtues excellent,
   None but for some and yet all different.
   O, mickle is the powerful grace that lies
   In herbs, plants, stones, and their true qualities:
   For nought so vile that on the earth doth live
   But to the earth some special good doth give,
   Nor aught so good but strain'd from that fair use
   Revolts from true birth, stumbling on abuse:
   Virtue itself turns vice, being misapplied;
   And vice sometimes by action dignified.
   Within the infant rind of this small flower
   Poison hath residence and medicine power:
   For this, being smelt, with that part cheers each part;
   Being tasted, slays all senses with the heart.
   Two such opposed kings encamp them still

In man as well as herbs, grace and rude will;
And where the worser is predominant,
Full soon the canker death eats up that plant.

Enter ROMEO

ROMEO
Good morrow, father.
FRIAR LAURENCE
Benedicite!
What early tongue so sweet saluteth me?
Young son, it argues a distemper'd head
So soon to bid good morrow to thy bed:
Care keeps his watch in every old man's eye,
And where care lodges, sleep will never lie;
But where unbruised youth with unstuff'd brain
Doth couch his limbs, there golden sleep doth reign:
Therefore thy earliness doth me assure
Thou art up-roused by some distemperature;
Or if not so, then here I hit it right,
Our Romeo hath not been in bed to-night.
ROMEO
That last is true; the sweeter rest was mine.
FRIAR LAURENCE
God pardon sin! wast thou with Rosaline?
ROMEO
With Rosaline, my ghostly father? no;
I have forgot that name, and that name's woe.
FRIAR LAURENCE
That's my good son: but where hast thou been, then?
ROMEO
I'll tell thee, ere thou ask it me again.
I have been feasting with mine enemy,
Where on a sudden one hath wounded me,
That's by me wounded: both our remedies

Within thy help and holy physic lies:
I bear no hatred, blessed man, for, lo,
My intercession likewise steads my foe.
FRIAR LAURENCE
Be plain, good son, and homely in thy drift;
Riddling confession finds but riddling shrift.
ROMEO
Then plainly know my heart's dear love is set
On the fair daughter of rich Capulet:
As mine on hers, so hers is set on mine;
And all combined, save what thou must combine
By holy marriage: when and where and how
We met, we woo'd and made exchange of vow,
I'll tell thee as we pass; but this I pray,
That thou consent to marry us to-day.
FRIAR LAURENCE
Holy Saint Francis, what a change is here!
Is Rosaline, whom thou didst love so dear,
So soon forsaken? young men's love then lies
Not truly in their hearts, but in their eyes.
Jesu Maria, what a deal of brine
Hath wash'd thy sallow cheeks for Rosaline!
How much salt water thrown away in waste,
To season love, that of it doth not taste!
The sun not yet thy sighs from heaven clears,
Thy old groans ring yet in my ancient ears;
Lo, here upon thy cheek the stain doth sit
Of an old tear that is not wash'd off yet:
If e'er thou wast thyself and these woes thine,
Thou and these woes were all for Rosaline:
And art thou changed? pronounce this sentence then,
Women may fall, when there's no strength in men.
ROMEO
Thou chid'st me oft for loving Rosaline.

FRIAR LAURENCE
For doting, not for loving, pupil mine.
ROMEO
And bad'st me bury love.
FRIAR LAURENCE
Not in a grave,
To lay one in, another out to have.
ROMEO
I pray thee, chide not; she whom I love now
Doth grace for grace and love for love allow;
The other did not so.
FRIAR LAURENCE
O, she knew well
Thy love did read by rote and could not spell.
But come, young waverer, come, go with me,
In one respect I'll thy assistant be;
For this alliance may so happy prove,
To turn your households' rancour to pure love.
ROMEO
O, let us hence; I stand on sudden haste.
FRIAR LAURENCE
Wisely and slow; they stumble that run fast.

Exeunt

SCENE IV.

A street.

Enter BENVOLIO and MERCUTIO

MERCUTIO
Where the devil should this Romeo be?
Came he not home to-night?
BENVOLIO
Not to his father's; I spoke with his man.

MERCUTIO
Ah, that same pale hard-hearted wench, that Rosaline.
Torments him so, that he will sure run mad.
BENVOLIO
Tybalt, the kinsman of old Capulet,
Hath sent a letter to his father's house.
MERCUTIO
A challenge, on my life.
BENVOLIO
Romeo will answer it.
MERCUTIO
Any man that can write may answer a letter.
BENVOLIO
Nay, he will answer the letter's master, how he
dares, being dared.
MERCUTIO
Alas poor Romeo! he is already dead; stabbed with a
white wench's black eye; shot through the ear with a
love-song; the very pin of his heart cleft with the
blind bow-boy's butt-shaft: and is he a man to
encounter Tybalt?
BENVOLIO
Why, what is Tybalt?
MERCUTIO
More than prince of cats, I can tell you. O, he is
the courageous captain of compliments. He fights as
you sing prick-song, keeps time, distance, and
proportion; rests me his minim rest, one, two, and
the third in your bosom: the very butcher of a silk
button, a duellist, a duellist; a gentleman of the
very first house, of the first and second cause:
ah, the immortal passado! the punto reverso! the
hai!
BENVOLIO

The what?
MERCUTIO
The pox of such antic, lisping, affecting
fantasticoes; these new tuners of accents! 'By Jesu,
a very good blade! a very tall man! a very good
whore!' Why, is not this a lamentable thing,
grandsire, that we should be thus afflicted with
these strange flies, these fashion-mongers, these
perdona-mi's, who stand so much on the new form,
that they cannot at ease on the old bench? O, their
bones, their bones!

Enter ROMEO

BENVOLIO
Here comes Romeo, here comes Romeo.
MERCUTIO
Without his roe, like a dried herring: flesh, flesh,
how art thou fishified! Now is he for the numbers
that Petrarch flowed in: Laura to his lady was but a
kitchen-wench; marry, she had a better love to
be-rhyme her; Dido a dowdy; Cleopatra a gipsy;
Helen and Hero hildings and harlots; Thisbe a grey
eye or so, but not to the purpose. Signior
Romeo, bon jour! there's a French salutation
to your French slop. You gave us the counterfeit
fairly last night.
ROMEO
Good morrow to you both. What counterfeit did I give
you?
MERCUTIO
The ship, sir, the slip; can you not conceive?
ROMEO
Pardon, good Mercutio, my business was great; and in
such a case as mine a man may strain courtesy.

MERCUTIO
That's as much as to say, such a case as yours
constrains a man to bow in the hams.
ROMEO
Meaning, to court'sy.
MERCUTIO
Thou hast most kindly hit it.
ROMEO
A most courteous exposition.
MERCUTIO
Nay, I am the very pink of courtesy.
ROMEO
Pink for flower.
MERCUTIO
Right.
ROMEO
Why, then is my pump well flowered.
MERCUTIO
Well said: follow me this jest now till thou hast
worn out thy pump, that when the single sole of it
is worn, the jest may remain after the wearing sole
singular.
ROMEO
O single-soled jest, solely singular for the
singleness.
MERCUTIO
Come between us, good Benvolio; my wits faint.
ROMEO
Switch and spurs, switch and spurs; or I'll cry a match.
MERCUTIO
Nay, if thy wits run the wild-goose chase, I have
done, for thou hast more of the wild-goose in one of
thy wits than, I am sure, I have in my whole five:
was I with you there for the goose?

ROMEO
Thou wast never with me for any thing when thou wast
not there for the goose.
MERCUTIO
I will bite thee by the ear for that jest.
ROMEO
Nay, good goose, bite not.
MERCUTIO
Thy wit is a very bitter sweeting; it is a most
sharp sauce.
ROMEO
And is it not well served in to a sweet goose?
MERCUTIO
O here's a wit of cheveril, that stretches from an
inch narrow to an ell broad!
ROMEO
I stretch it out for that word 'broad;' which added
to the goose, proves thee far and wide a broad goose.
MERCUTIO
Why, is not this better now than groaning for love?
now art thou sociable, now art thou Romeo; now art
thou what thou art, by art as well as by nature:
for this drivelling love is like a great natural,
that runs lolling up and down to hide his bauble in a
hole.
BENVOLIO
Stop there, stop there.
MERCUTIO
Thou desirest me to stop in my tale against the hair.
BENVOLIO
Thou wouldst else have made thy tale large.
MERCUTIO
O, thou art deceived; I would have made it short:
for I was come to the whole depth of my tale; and

meant, indeed, to occupy the argument no longer.
ROMEO
Here's goodly gear!

Enter Nurse and PETER

MERCUTIO
A sail, a sail!
BENVOLIO
Two, two; a shirt and a smock.
Nurse
Peter!
PETER
Anon!
Nurse
My fan, Peter.
MERCUTIO
Good Peter, to hide her face; for her fan's the
fairer face.
Nurse
God ye good morrow, gentlemen.
MERCUTIO
God ye good den, fair gentlewoman.
Nurse
Is it good den?
MERCUTIO
'Tis no less, I tell you, for the bawdy hand of the
dial is now upon the prick of noon.
Nurse
Out upon you! what a man are you!
ROMEO
One, gentlewoman, that God hath made for himself to
mar.
Nurse
By my troth, it is well said; 'for himself to mar,'

quoth a'? Gentlemen, can any of you tell me where I
may find the young Romeo?
ROMEO
I can tell you; but young Romeo will be older when
you have found him than he was when you sought him:
I am the youngest of that name, for fault of a worse.
Nurse
You say well.
MERCUTIO
Yea, is the worst well? very well took, i' faith;
wisely, wisely.
Nurse
if you be he, sir, I desire some confidence with
you.
BENVOLIO
She will indite him to some supper.
MERCUTIO
A bawd, a bawd, a bawd! so ho!
ROMEO
What hast thou found?
MERCUTIO
No hare, sir; unless a hare, sir, in a lenten pie,
that is something stale and hoar ere it be spent.

Sings

An old hare hoar,
And an old hare hoar,
Is very good meat in lent
But a hare that is hoar
Is too much for a score,
When it hoars ere it be spent.
Romeo, will you come to your father's? we'll
to dinner, thither.
ROMEO

I will follow you.
MERCUTIO
Farewell, ancient lady; farewell,

Singing

'lady, lady, lady.'

Exeunt MERCUTIO and BENVOLIO

Nurse
Marry, farewell! I pray you, sir, what saucy
merchant was this, that was so full of his ropery?
ROMEO
A gentleman, nurse, that loves to hear himself talk,
and will speak more in a minute than he will stand
to in a month.
Nurse
An a' speak any thing against me, I'll take him
down, an a' were lustier than he is, and twenty such
Jacks; and if I cannot, I'll find those that shall.
Scurvy knave! I am none of his flirt-gills; I am
none of his skains-mates. And thou must stand by
too, and suffer every knave to use me at his pleasure?
PETER
I saw no man use you a pleasure; if I had, my weapon
should quickly have been out, I warrant you: I dare
draw as soon as another man, if I see occasion in a
good quarrel, and the law on my side.
Nurse
Now, afore God, I am so vexed, that every part about
me quivers. Scurvy knave! Pray you, sir, a word:
and as I told you, my young lady bade me inquire you
out; what she bade me say, I will keep to myself:
but first let me tell ye, if ye should lead her into

a fool's paradise, as they say, it were a very gross
kind of behavior, as they say: for the gentlewoman
is young; and, therefore, if you should deal double
with her, truly it were an ill thing to be offered
to any gentlewoman, and very weak dealing.

ROMEO

Nurse, commend me to thy lady and mistress. I
protest unto thee--

Nurse

Good heart, and, i' faith, I will tell her as much:
Lord, Lord, she will be a joyful woman.

ROMEO

What wilt thou tell her, nurse? thou dost not mark me.

Nurse

I will tell her, sir, that you do protest; which, as
I take it, is a gentlemanlike offer.

ROMEO

Bid her devise
Some means to come to shrift this afternoon;
And there she shall at Friar Laurence' cell
Be shrived and married. Here is for thy pains.

Nurse

No truly sir; not a penny.

ROMEO

Go to; I say you shall.

Nurse

This afternoon, sir? well, she shall be there.

ROMEO

And stay, good nurse, behind the abbey wall:
Within this hour my man shall be with thee
And bring thee cords made like a tackled stair;
Which to the high top-gallant of my joy
Must be my convoy in the secret night.
Farewell; be trusty, and I'll quit thy pains:

Farewell; commend me to thy mistress.
Nurse
Now God in heaven bless thee! Hark you, sir.
ROMEO
What say'st thou, my dear nurse?
Nurse
Is your man secret? Did you ne'er hear say,
Two may keep counsel, putting one away?
ROMEO
I warrant thee, my man's as true as steel.
NURSE
Well, sir; my mistress is the sweetest lady--Lord,
Lord! when 'twas a little prating thing:--O, there
is a nobleman in town, one Paris, that would fain
lay knife aboard; but she, good soul, had as lief
see a toad, a very toad, as see him. I anger her
sometimes and tell her that Paris is the properer
man; but, I'll warrant you, when I say so, she looks
as pale as any clout in the versal world. Doth not
rosemary and Romeo begin both with a letter?
ROMEO
Ay, nurse; what of that? both with an R.
Nurse
Ah. mocker! that's the dog's name; R is for
the--No; I know it begins with some other
letter:--and she hath the prettiest sententious of
it, of you and rosemary, that it would do you good
to hear it.
ROMEO
Commend me to thy lady.
Nurse
Ay, a thousand times.

Exit Romeo

Peter!
PETER
Anon!
Nurse
Peter, take my fan, and go before and apace.

Exeunt

SCENE V.

Capulet's orchard.

Enter JULIET

JULIET
The clock struck nine when I did send the nurse;
In half an hour she promised to return.
Perchance she cannot meet him: that's not so.
O, she is lame! love's heralds should be thoughts,
Which ten times faster glide than the sun's beams,
Driving back shadows over louring hills:
Therefore do nimble-pinion'd doves draw love,
And therefore hath the wind-swift Cupid wings.
Now is the sun upon the highmost hill
Of this day's journey, and from nine till twelve
Is three long hours, yet she is not come.
Had she affections and warm youthful blood,
She would be as swift in motion as a ball;
My words would bandy her to my sweet love,
And his to me:
But old folks, many feign as they were dead;
Unwieldy, slow, heavy and pale as lead.
O God, she comes!

Enter Nurse and PETER

O honey nurse, what news?
Hast thou met with him? Send thy man away.
Nurse
Peter, stay at the gate.

Exit PETER

JULIET
Now, good sweet nurse,--O Lord, why look'st thou sad?
Though news be sad, yet tell them merrily;
If good, thou shamest the music of sweet news
By playing it to me with so sour a face.
Nurse
I am a-weary, give me leave awhile:
Fie, how my bones ache! what a jaunt have I had!
JULIET
I would thou hadst my bones, and I thy news:
Nay, come, I pray thee, speak; good, good nurse, speak.
Nurse
Jesu, what haste? can you not stay awhile?
Do you not see that I am out of breath?
JULIET
How art thou out of breath, when thou hast breath
To say to me that thou art out of breath?
The excuse that thou dost make in this delay
Is longer than the tale thou dost excuse.
Is thy news good, or bad? answer to that;
Say either, and I'll stay the circumstance:
Let me be satisfied, is't good or bad?
Nurse
Well, you have made a simple choice; you know not
how to choose a man: Romeo! no, not he; though his
face be better than any man's, yet his leg excels
all men's; and for a hand, and a foot, and a body,
though they be not to be talked on, yet they are

past compare: he is not the flower of courtesy,
but, I'll warrant him, as gentle as a lamb. Go thy
ways, wench; serve God. What, have you dined at
home?

JULIET
No, no: but all this did I know before.
What says he of our marriage? what of that?

Nurse
Lord, how my head aches! what a head have I!
It beats as it would fall in twenty pieces.
My back o' t' other side,--O, my back, my back!
Beshrew your heart for sending me about,
To catch my death with jaunting up and down!

JULIET
I' faith, I am sorry that thou art not well.
Sweet, sweet, sweet nurse, tell me, what says my love?

Nurse
Your love says, like an honest gentleman, and a
courteous, and a kind, and a handsome, and, I
warrant, a virtuous,--Where is your mother?

JULIET
Where is my mother! why, she is within;
Where should she be? How oddly thou repliest!
'Your love says, like an honest gentleman,
Where is your mother?'

Nurse
O God's lady dear!
Are you so hot? marry, come up, I trow;
Is this the poultice for my aching bones?
Henceforward do your messages yourself.

JULIET
Here's such a coil! come, what says Romeo?

Nurse
Have you got leave to go to shrift to-day?

JULIET
  I have.
Nurse
  Then hie you hence to Friar Laurence' cell;
  There stays a husband to make you a wife:
  Now comes the wanton blood up in your cheeks,
  They'll be in scarlet straight at any news.
  Hie you to church; I must another way,
  To fetch a ladder, by the which your love
  Must climb a bird's nest soon when it is dark:
  I am the drudge and toil in your delight,
  But you shall bear the burden soon at night.
  Go; I'll to dinner: hie you to the cell.
JULIET
  Hie to high fortune! Honest nurse, farewell.

Exeunt

SCENE VI.

Friar Laurence's cell.

Enter FRIAR LAURENCE and ROMEO

FRIAR LAURENCE
  So smile the heavens upon this holy act,
  That after hours with sorrow chide us not!
ROMEO
  Amen, amen! but come what sorrow can,
  It cannot countervail the exchange of joy
  That one short minute gives me in her sight:
  Do thou but close our hands with holy words,
  Then love-devouring death do what he dare;
  It is enough I may but call her mine.
FRIAR LAURENCE
  These violent delights have violent ends

And in their triumph die, like fire and powder,
Which as they kiss consume: the sweetest honey
Is loathsome in his own deliciousness
And in the taste confounds the appetite:
Therefore love moderately; long love doth so;
Too swift arrives as tardy as too slow.

Enter JULIET
Here comes the lady: O, so light a foot
Will ne'er wear out the everlasting flint:
A lover may bestride the gossamer
That idles in the wanton summer air,
And yet not fall; so light is vanity.
JULIET
Good even to my ghostly confessor.
FRIAR LAURENCE
Romeo shall thank thee, daughter, for us both.
JULIET
As much to him, else is his thanks too much.
ROMEO
Ah, Juliet, if the measure of thy joy
Be heap'd like mine and that thy skill be more
To blazon it, then sweeten with thy breath
This neighbour air, and let rich music's tongue
Unfold the imagined happiness that both
Receive in either by this dear encounter.
JULIET
Conceit, more rich in matter than in words,
Brags of his substance, not of ornament:
They are but beggars that can count their worth;
But my true love is grown to such excess
I cannot sum up sum of half my wealth.
FRIAR LAURENCE
Come, come with me, and we will make short work;
For, by your leaves, you shall not stay alone

Till holy church incorporate two in one.

Exeunt

ACT III

SCENE I.

A public place.

Enter MERCUTIO, BENVOLIO, Page, and Servants

BENVOLIO
I pray thee, good Mercutio, let's retire:
The day is hot, the Capulets abroad,
And, if we meet, we shall not scape a brawl;
For now, these hot days, is the mad blood stirring.
MERCUTIO
Thou art like one of those fellows that when he
enters the confines of a tavern claps me his sword
upon the table and says 'God send me no need of
thee!' and by the operation of the second cup draws
it on the drawer, when indeed there is no need.
BENVOLIO
Am I like such a fellow?
MERCUTIO
Come, come, thou art as hot a Jack in thy mood as
any in Italy, and as soon moved to be moody, and as
soon moody to be moved.
BENVOLIO
And what to?
MERCUTIO
Nay, an there were two such, we should have none
shortly, for one would kill the other. Thou! why,
thou wilt quarrel with a man that hath a hair more,
or a hair less, in his beard, than thou hast: thou
wilt quarrel with a man for cracking nuts, having no
other reason but because thou hast hazel eyes: what
eye but such an eye would spy out such a quarrel?

Thy head is as fun of quarrels as an egg is full of
meat, and yet thy head hath been beaten as addle as
an egg for quarrelling: thou hast quarrelled with a
man for coughing in the street, because he hath
wakened thy dog that hath lain asleep in the sun:
didst thou not fall out with a tailor for wearing
his new doublet before Easter? with another, for
tying his new shoes with old riband? and yet thou
wilt tutor me from quarrelling!
BENVOLIO
An I were so apt to quarrel as thou art, any man
should buy the fee-simple of my life for an hour and a
quarter.
MERCUTIO
The fee-simple! O simple!
BENVOLIO
By my head, here come the Capulets.
MERCUTIO
By my heel, I care not.

Enter TYBALT and others

TYBALT
Follow me close, for I will speak to them.
Gentlemen, good den: a word with one of you.
MERCUTIO
And but one word with one of us? couple it with
something; make it a word and a blow.
TYBALT
You shall find me apt enough to that, sir, an you
will give me occasion.
MERCUTIO
Could you not take some occasion without giving?
TYBALT
Mercutio, thou consort'st with Romeo,--

MERCUTIO
Consort! what, dost thou make us minstrels? an
thou make minstrels of us, look to hear nothing but
discords: here's my fiddlestick; here's that shall
make you dance. 'Zounds, consort!
BENVOLIO
We talk here in the public haunt of men:
Either withdraw unto some private place,
And reason coldly of your grievances,
Or else depart; here all eyes gaze on us.
MERCUTIO
Men's eyes were made to look, and let them gaze;
I will not budge for no man's pleasure, I.

Enter ROMEO

TYBALT
Well, peace be with you, sir: here comes my man.
MERCUTIO
But I'll be hanged, sir, if he wear your livery:
Marry, go before to field, he'll be your follower;
Your worship in that sense may call him 'man.'
TYBALT
Romeo, the hate I bear thee can afford
No better term than this,--thou art a villain.
ROMEO
Tybalt, the reason that I have to love thee
Doth much excuse the appertaining rage
To such a greeting: villain am I none;
Therefore farewell; I see thou know'st me not.
TYBALT
Boy, this shall not excuse the injuries
That thou hast done me; therefore turn and draw.
ROMEO
I do protest, I never injured thee,

But love thee better than thou canst devise,
Till thou shalt know the reason of my love:
And so, good Capulet,--which name I tender
As dearly as my own,--be satisfied.
MERCUTIO
O calm, dishonourable, vile submission!
Alla stoccata carries it away.

Draws

Tybalt, you rat-catcher, will you walk?
TYBALT
What wouldst thou have with me?
MERCUTIO
Good king of cats, nothing but one of your nine
lives; that I mean to make bold withal, and as you
shall use me hereafter, drybeat the rest of the
eight. Will you pluck your sword out of his pitcher
by the ears? make haste, lest mine be about your
ears ere it be out.
TYBALT
I am for you.

Drawing

ROMEO
Gentle Mercutio, put thy rapier up.
MERCUTIO
Come, sir, your passado.

They fight

ROMEO
Draw, Benvolio; beat down their weapons.
Gentlemen, for shame, forbear this outrage!
Tybalt, Mercutio, the prince expressly hath

Romeo and Juliet — Act III

Forbidden bandying in Verona streets:
Hold, Tybalt! good Mercutio!

*TYBALT under ROMEO's arm stabs MERCUTIO, and flies
with his followers*

MERCUTIO
I am hurt.
A plague o' both your houses! I am sped.
Is he gone, and hath nothing?
BENVOLIO
What, art thou hurt?
MERCUTIO
Ay, ay, a scratch, a scratch; marry, 'tis enough.
Where is my page? Go, villain, fetch a surgeon.

Exit Page

ROMEO
Courage, man; the hurt cannot be much.
MERCUTIO
No, 'tis not so deep as a well, nor so wide as a
church-door; but 'tis enough,'twill serve: ask for
me to-morrow, and you shall find me a grave man. I
am peppered, I warrant, for this world. A plague o'
both your houses! 'Zounds, a dog, a rat, a mouse, a
cat, to scratch a man to death! a braggart, a
rogue, a villain, that fights by the book of
arithmetic! Why the devil came you between us? I
was hurt under your arm.
ROMEO
I thought all for the best.
MERCUTIO
Help me into some house, Benvolio,
Or I shall faint. A plague o' both your houses!

Romeo and Juliet — Act III

They have made worms' meat of me: I have it,
And soundly too: your houses!

Exeunt MERCUTIO and BENVOLIO

ROMEO
This gentleman, the prince's near ally,
My very friend, hath got his mortal hurt
In my behalf; my reputation stain'd
With Tybalt's slander,--Tybalt, that an hour
Hath been my kinsman! O sweet Juliet,
Thy beauty hath made me effeminate
And in my temper soften'd valour's steel!

Re-enter BENVOLIO

BENVOLIO
O Romeo, Romeo, brave Mercutio's dead!
That gallant spirit hath aspired the clouds,
Which too untimely here did scorn the earth.
ROMEO
This day's black fate on more days doth depend;
This but begins the woe, others must end.
BENVOLIO
Here comes the furious Tybalt back again.
ROMEO
Alive, in triumph! and Mercutio slain!
Away to heaven, respective lenity,
And fire-eyed fury be my conduct now!

Re-enter TYBALT

Now, Tybalt, take the villain back again,
That late thou gavest me; for Mercutio's soul
Is but a little way above our heads,
Staying for thine to keep him company:

73

Either thou, or I, or both, must go with him.
TYBALT
Thou, wretched boy, that didst consort him here,
Shalt with him hence.
ROMEO
This shall determine that.

They fight; TYBALT falls

BENVOLIO
Romeo, away, be gone!
The citizens are up, and Tybalt slain.
Stand not amazed: the prince will doom thee death,
If thou art taken: hence, be gone, away!
ROMEO
O, I am fortune's fool!
BENVOLIO
Why dost thou stay?

Exit ROMEO

Enter Citizens, & c

First Citizen
Which way ran he that kill'd Mercutio?
Tybalt, that murderer, which way ran he?
BENVOLIO
There lies that Tybalt.
First Citizen
Up, sir, go with me;
I charge thee in the princes name, obey.

*Enter Prince, attended; MONTAGUE, CAPULET, their
Wives, and others*

PRINCE

Where are the vile beginners of this fray?
BENVOLIO
O noble prince, I can discover all
The unlucky manage of this fatal brawl:
There lies the man, slain by young Romeo,
That slew thy kinsman, brave Mercutio.
LADY CAPULET
Tybalt, my cousin! O my brother's child!
O prince! O cousin! husband! O, the blood is spilt
O my dear kinsman! Prince, as thou art true,
For blood of ours, shed blood of Montague.
O cousin, cousin!
PRINCE
Benvolio, who began this bloody fray?
BENVOLIO
Tybalt, here slain, whom Romeo's hand did slay;
Romeo that spoke him fair, bade him bethink
How nice the quarrel was, and urged withal
Your high displeasure: all this uttered
With gentle breath, calm look, knees humbly bow'd,
Could not take truce with the unruly spleen
Of Tybalt deaf to peace, but that he tilts
With piercing steel at bold Mercutio's breast,
Who all as hot, turns deadly point to point,
And, with a martial scorn, with one hand beats
Cold death aside, and with the other sends
It back to Tybalt, whose dexterity,
Retorts it: Romeo he cries aloud,
'Hold, friends! friends, part!' and, swifter than
his tongue,
His agile arm beats down their fatal points,
And 'twixt them rushes; underneath whose arm
An envious thrust from Tybalt hit the life
Of stout Mercutio, and then Tybalt fled;

But by and by comes back to Romeo,
Who had but newly entertain'd revenge,
And to 't they go like lightning, for, ere I
Could draw to part them, was stout Tybalt slain.
And, as he fell, did Romeo turn and fly.
This is the truth, or let Benvolio die.

LADY CAPULET
He is a kinsman to the Montague;
Affection makes him false; he speaks not true:
Some twenty of them fought in this black strife,
And all those twenty could but kill one life.
I beg for justice, which thou, prince, must give;
Romeo slew Tybalt, Romeo must not live.

PRINCE
Romeo slew him, he slew Mercutio;
Who now the price of his dear blood doth owe?

MONTAGUE
Not Romeo, prince, he was Mercutio's friend;
His fault concludes but what the law should end,
The life of Tybalt.

PRINCE
And for that offence
Immediately we do exile him hence:
I have an interest in your hate's proceeding,
My blood for your rude brawls doth lie a-bleeding;
But I'll amerce you with so strong a fine
That you shall all repent the loss of mine:
I will be deaf to pleading and excuses;
Nor tears nor prayers shall purchase out abuses:
Therefore use none: let Romeo hence in haste,
Else, when he's found, that hour is his last.
Bear hence this body and attend our will:
Mercy but murders, pardoning those that kill.

Exeunt

SCENE II.

Capulet's orchard.

Enter JULIET

JULIET

Gallop apace, you fiery-footed steeds,
Towards Phoebus' lodging: such a wagoner
As Phaethon would whip you to the west,
And bring in cloudy night immediately.
Spread thy close curtain, love-performing night,
That runaway's eyes may wink and Romeo
Leap to these arms, untalk'd of and unseen.
Lovers can see to do their amorous rites
By their own beauties; or, if love be blind,
It best agrees with night. Come, civil night,
Thou sober-suited matron, all in black,
And learn me how to lose a winning match,
Play'd for a pair of stainless maidenhoods:
Hood my unmann'd blood, bating in my cheeks,
With thy black mantle; till strange love, grown bold,
Think true love acted simple modesty.
Come, night; come, Romeo; come, thou day in night;
For thou wilt lie upon the wings of night
Whiter than new snow on a raven's back.
Come, gentle night, come, loving, black-brow'd night,
Give me my Romeo; and, when he shall die,
Take him and cut him out in little stars,
And he will make the face of heaven so fine
That all the world will be in love with night
And pay no worship to the garish sun.
O, I have bought the mansion of a love,
But not possess'd it, and, though I am sold,

Not yet enjoy'd: so tedious is this day
As is the night before some festival
To an impatient child that hath new robes
And may not wear them. O, here comes my nurse,
And she brings news; and every tongue that speaks
But Romeo's name speaks heavenly eloquence.

Enter Nurse, with cords

Now, nurse, what news? What hast thou there? the cords
That Romeo bid thee fetch?
Nurse
Ay, ay, the cords.

Throws them down

JULIET
Ay me! what news? why dost thou wring thy hands?
Nurse
Ah, well-a-day! he's dead, he's dead, he's dead!
We are undone, lady, we are undone!
Alack the day! he's gone, he's kill'd, he's dead!
JULIET
Can heaven be so envious?
Nurse
Romeo can,
Though heaven cannot: O Romeo, Romeo!
Who ever would have thought it? Romeo!
JULIET
What devil art thou, that dost torment me thus?
This torture should be roar'd in dismal hell.
Hath Romeo slain himself? say thou but 'I,'
And that bare vowel 'I' shall poison more
Than the death-darting eye of cockatrice:
I am not I, if there be such an I;

Or those eyes shut, that make thee answer 'I.'
If he be slain, say 'I'; or if not, no:
Brief sounds determine of my weal or woe.
Nurse
I saw the wound, I saw it with mine eyes,--
God save the mark!--here on his manly breast:
A piteous corse, a bloody piteous corse;
Pale, pale as ashes, all bedaub'd in blood,
All in gore-blood; I swounded at the sight.
JULIET
O, break, my heart! poor bankrupt, break at once!
To prison, eyes, ne'er look on liberty!
Vile earth, to earth resign; end motion here;
And thou and Romeo press one heavy bier!
Nurse
O Tybalt, Tybalt, the best friend I had!
O courteous Tybalt! honest gentleman!
That ever I should live to see thee dead!
JULIET
What storm is this that blows so contrary?
Is Romeo slaughter'd, and is Tybalt dead?
My dear-loved cousin, and my dearer lord?
Then, dreadful trumpet, sound the general doom!
For who is living, if those two are gone?
Nurse
Tybalt is gone, and Romeo banished;
Romeo that kill'd him, he is banished.
JULIET
O God! did Romeo's hand shed Tybalt's blood?
Nurse
It did, it did; alas the day, it did!
JULIET
O serpent heart, hid with a flowering face!
Did ever dragon keep so fair a cave?

Beautiful tyrant! fiend angelical!
Dove-feather'd raven! wolvish-ravening lamb!
Despised substance of divinest show!
Just opposite to what thou justly seem'st,
A damned saint, an honourable villain!
O nature, what hadst thou to do in hell,
When thou didst bower the spirit of a fiend
In moral paradise of such sweet flesh?
Was ever book containing such vile matter
So fairly bound? O that deceit should dwell
In such a gorgeous palace!

Nurse

There's no trust,
No faith, no honesty in men; all perjured,
All forsworn, all naught, all dissemblers.
Ah, where's my man? give me some aqua vitae:
These griefs, these woes, these sorrows make me old.
Shame come to Romeo!

JULIET

Blister'd be thy tongue
For such a wish! he was not born to shame:
Upon his brow shame is ashamed to sit;
For 'tis a throne where honour may be crown'd
Sole monarch of the universal earth.
O, what a beast was I to chide at him!

Nurse

Will you speak well of him that kill'd your cousin?

JULIET

Shall I speak ill of him that is my husband?
Ah, poor my lord, what tongue shall smooth thy name,
When I, thy three-hours wife, have mangled it?
But, wherefore, villain, didst thou kill my cousin?
That villain cousin would have kill'd my husband:
Back, foolish tears, back to your native spring;

80

Romeo and Juliet — Act III

Your tributary drops belong to woe,
Which you, mistaking, offer up to joy.
My husband lives, that Tybalt would have slain;
And Tybalt's dead, that would have slain my husband:
All this is comfort; wherefore weep I then?
Some word there was, worser than Tybalt's death,
That murder'd me: I would forget it fain;
But, O, it presses to my memory,
Like damned guilty deeds to sinners' minds:
'Tybalt is dead, and Romeo--banished;'
That 'banished,' that one word 'banished,'
Hath slain ten thousand Tybalts. Tybalt's death
Was woe enough, if it had ended there:
Or, if sour woe delights in fellowship
And needly will be rank'd with other griefs,
Why follow'd not, when she said 'Tybalt's dead,'
Thy father, or thy mother, nay, or both,
Which modern lamentations might have moved?
But with a rear-ward following Tybalt's death,
'Romeo is banished,' to speak that word,
Is father, mother, Tybalt, Romeo, Juliet,
All slain, all dead. 'Romeo is banished!'
There is no end, no limit, measure, bound,
In that word's death; no words can that woe sound.
Where is my father, and my mother, nurse?
Nurse
Weeping and wailing over Tybalt's corse:
Will you go to them? I will bring you thither.
JULIET
Wash they his wounds with tears: mine shall be spent,
When theirs are dry, for Romeo's banishment.
Take up those cords: poor ropes, you are beguiled,
Both you and I; for Romeo is exiled:
He made you for a highway to my bed;

81

But I, a maid, die maiden-widowed.
Come, cords, come, nurse; I'll to my wedding-bed;
And death, not Romeo, take my maidenhead!
Nurse
Hie to your chamber: I'll find Romeo
To comfort you: I wot well where he is.
Hark ye, your Romeo will be here at night:
I'll to him; he is hid at Laurence' cell.
JULIET
O, find him! give this ring to my true knight,
And bid him come to take his last farewell.

Exeunt

SCENE III.

Friar Laurence's cell.

Enter FRIAR LAURENCE

FRIAR LAURENCE
Romeo, come forth; come forth, thou fearful man:
Affliction is enamour'd of thy parts,
And thou art wedded to calamity.

Enter ROMEO

ROMEO
Father, what news? what is the prince's doom?
What sorrow craves acquaintance at my hand,
That I yet know not?
FRIAR LAURENCE
Too familiar
Is my dear son with such sour company:
I bring thee tidings of the prince's doom.
ROMEO

What less than dooms-day is the prince's doom?
FRIAR LAURENCE
A gentler judgment vanish'd from his lips,
Not body's death, but body's banishment.
ROMEO
Ha, banishment! be merciful, say 'death;'
For exile hath more terror in his look,
Much more than death: do not say 'banishment.'
FRIAR LAURENCE
Hence from Verona art thou banished:
Be patient, for the world is broad and wide.
ROMEO
There is no world without Verona walls,
But purgatory, torture, hell itself.
Hence-banished is banish'd from the world,
And world's exile is death: then banished,
Is death mis-term'd: calling death banishment,
Thou cutt'st my head off with a golden axe,
And smilest upon the stroke that murders me.
FRIAR LAURENCE
O deadly sin! O rude unthankfulness!
Thy fault our law calls death; but the kind prince,
Taking thy part, hath rush'd aside the law,
And turn'd that black word death to banishment:
This is dear mercy, and thou seest it not.
ROMEO
'Tis torture, and not mercy: heaven is here,
Where Juliet lives; and every cat and dog
And little mouse, every unworthy thing,
Live here in heaven and may look on her;
But Romeo may not: more validity,
More honourable state, more courtship lives
In carrion-flies than Romeo: they my seize
On the white wonder of dear Juliet's hand

And steal immortal blessing from her lips,
Who even in pure and vestal modesty,
Still blush, as thinking their own kisses sin;
But Romeo may not; he is banished:
Flies may do this, but I from this must fly:
They are free men, but I am banished.
And say'st thou yet that exile is not death?
Hadst thou no poison mix'd, no sharp-ground knife,
No sudden mean of death, though ne'er so mean,
But 'banished' to kill me?--'banished'?
O friar, the damned use that word in hell;
Howlings attend it: how hast thou the heart,
Being a divine, a ghostly confessor,
A sin-absolver, and my friend profess'd,
To mangle me with that word 'banished'?
FRIAR LAURENCE
Thou fond mad man, hear me but speak a word.
ROMEO
O, thou wilt speak again of banishment.
FRIAR LAURENCE
I'll give thee armour to keep off that word:
Adversity's sweet milk, philosophy,
To comfort thee, though thou art banished.
ROMEO
Yet 'banished'? Hang up philosophy!
Unless philosophy can make a Juliet,
Displant a town, reverse a prince's doom,
It helps not, it prevails not: talk no more.
FRIAR LAURENCE
O, then I see that madmen have no ears.
ROMEO
How should they, when that wise men have no eyes?
FRIAR LAURENCE
Let me dispute with thee of thy estate.

ROMEO
Thou canst not speak of that thou dost not feel:
Wert thou as young as I, Juliet thy love,
An hour but married, Tybalt murdered,
Doting like me and like me banished,
Then mightst thou speak, then mightst thou tear thy hair,
And fall upon the ground, as I do now,
Taking the measure of an unmade grave.

Knocking within

FRIAR LAURENCE
Arise; one knocks; good Romeo, hide thyself.
ROMEO
Not I; unless the breath of heartsick groans,
Mist-like, infold me from the search of eyes.

Knocking

FRIAR LAURENCE
Hark, how they knock! Who's there? Romeo, arise;
Thou wilt be taken. Stay awhile! Stand up;
Knocking

Run to my study. By and by! God's will,
What simpleness is this! I come, I come!

Knocking

Who knocks so hard? whence come you? what's your
will?
Nurse
[Within] Let me come in, and you shall know
my errand;
I come from Lady Juliet.
FRIAR LAURENCE

Welcome, then.

Enter Nurse

Nurse
　O holy friar, O, tell me, holy friar,
　Where is my lady's lord, where's Romeo?
FRIAR LAURENCE
　There on the ground, with his own tears made drunk.
Nurse
　O, he is even in my mistress' case,
　Just in her case! O woful sympathy!
　Piteous predicament! Even so lies she,
　Blubbering and weeping, weeping and blubbering.
　Stand up, stand up; stand, and you be a man:
　For Juliet's sake, for her sake, rise and stand;
　Why should you fall into so deep an O?
ROMEO
　Nurse!
Nurse
　Ah sir! ah sir! Well, death's the end of all.
ROMEO
　Spakest thou of Juliet? how is it with her?
　Doth she not think me an old murderer,
　Now I have stain'd the childhood of our joy
　With blood removed but little from her own?
　Where is she? and how doth she? and what says
　My conceal'd lady to our cancell'd love?
Nurse
　O, she says nothing, sir, but weeps and weeps;
　And now falls on her bed; and then starts up,
　And Tybalt calls; and then on Romeo cries,
　And then down falls again.
ROMEO
　As if that name,

Shot from the deadly level of a gun,
Did murder her; as that name's cursed hand
Murder'd her kinsman. O, tell me, friar, tell me,
In what vile part of this anatomy
Doth my name lodge? tell me, that I may sack
The hateful mansion.

Drawing his sword

FRIAR LAURENCE
Hold thy desperate hand:
Art thou a man? thy form cries out thou art:
Thy tears are womanish; thy wild acts denote
The unreasonable fury of a beast:
Unseemly woman in a seeming man!
Or ill-beseeming beast in seeming both!
Thou hast amazed me: by my holy order,
I thought thy disposition better temper'd.
Hast thou slain Tybalt? wilt thou slay thyself?
And stay thy lady too that lives in thee,
By doing damned hate upon thyself?
Why rail'st thou on thy birth, the heaven, and earth?
Since birth, and heaven, and earth, all three do meet
In thee at once; which thou at once wouldst lose.
Fie, fie, thou shamest thy shape, thy love, thy wit;
Which, like a usurer, abound'st in all,
And usest none in that true use indeed
Which should bedeck thy shape, thy love, thy wit:
Thy noble shape is but a form of wax,
Digressing from the valour of a man;
Thy dear love sworn but hollow perjury,
Killing that love which thou hast vow'd to cherish;
Thy wit, that ornament to shape and love,
Misshapen in the conduct of them both,
Like powder in a skitless soldier's flask,

Is set afire by thine own ignorance,
And thou dismember'd with thine own defence.
What, rouse thee, man! thy Juliet is alive,
For whose dear sake thou wast but lately dead;
There art thou happy: Tybalt would kill thee,
But thou slew'st Tybalt; there are thou happy too:
The law that threaten'd death becomes thy friend
And turns it to exile; there art thou happy:
A pack of blessings lights up upon thy back;
Happiness courts thee in her best array;
But, like a misbehaved and sullen wench,
Thou pout'st upon thy fortune and thy love:
Take heed, take heed, for such die miserable.
Go, get thee to thy love, as was decreed,
Ascend her chamber, hence and comfort her:
But look thou stay not till the watch be set,
For then thou canst not pass to Mantua;
Where thou shalt live, till we can find a time
To blaze your marriage, reconcile your friends,
Beg pardon of the prince, and call thee back
With twenty hundred thousand times more joy
Than thou went'st forth in lamentation.
Go before, nurse: commend me to thy lady;
And bid her hasten all the house to bed,
Which heavy sorrow makes them apt unto:
Romeo is coming.

Nurse

O Lord, I could have stay'd here all the night
To hear good counsel: O, what learning is!
My lord, I'll tell my lady you will come.

ROMEO

Do so, and bid my sweet prepare to chide.

Nurse

Here, sir, a ring she bid me give you, sir:

Hie you, make haste, for it grows very late.

Exit

ROMEO
How well my comfort is revived by this!
FRIAR LAURENCE
Go hence; good night; and here stands all your state:
Either be gone before the watch be set,
Or by the break of day disguised from hence:
Sojourn in Mantua; I'll find out your man,
And he shall signify from time to time
Every good hap to you that chances here:
Give me thy hand; 'tis late: farewell; good night.
ROMEO
But that a joy past joy calls out on me,
It were a grief, so brief to part with thee: Farewell.

Exeunt

SCENE IV.

A room in Capulet's house.

Enter CAPULET, LADY CAPULET, and PARIS

CAPULET
Things have fall'n out, sir, so unluckily,
That we have had no time to move our daughter:
Look you, she loved her kinsman Tybalt dearly,
And so did I:--Well, we were born to die.
'Tis very late, she'll not come down to-night:
I promise you, but for your company,
I would have been a-bed an hour ago.
PARIS
These times of woe afford no time to woo.
Madam, good night: commend me to your daughter.
LADY CAPULET

I will, and know her mind early to-morrow;
To-night she is mew'd up to her heaviness.
CAPULET
    Sir Paris, I will make a desperate tender
    Of my child's love: I think she will be ruled
    In all respects by me; nay, more, I doubt it not.
    Wife, go you to her ere you go to bed;
    Acquaint her here of my son Paris' love;
    And bid her, mark you me, on Wednesday next--
    But, soft! what day is this?
PARIS
    Monday, my lord,
CAPULET
    Monday! ha, ha! Well, Wednesday is too soon,
    O' Thursday let it be: o' Thursday, tell her,
    She shall be married to this noble earl.
    Will you be ready? do you like this haste?
    We'll keep no great ado,--a friend or two;
    For, hark you, Tybalt being slain so late,
    It may be thought we held him carelessly,
    Being our kinsman, if we revel much:
    Therefore we'll have some half a dozen friends,
    And there an end. But what say you to Thursday?
PARIS
    My lord, I would that Thursday were to-morrow.
CAPULET
    Well get you gone: o' Thursday be it, then.
    Go you to Juliet ere you go to bed,
    Prepare her, wife, against this wedding-day.
    Farewell, my lord. Light to my chamber, ho!
    Afore me! it is so very very late,
    That we may call it early by and by.
    Good night.

Exeunt

SCENE V.

Capulet's orchard.

Enter ROMEO and JULIET above, at the window

JULIET

Wilt thou be gone? it is not yet near day:
It was the nightingale, and not the lark,
That pierced the fearful hollow of thine ear;
Nightly she sings on yon pomegranate-tree:
Believe me, love, it was the nightingale.

ROMEO

It was the lark, the herald of the morn,
No nightingale: look, love, what envious streaks
Do lace the severing clouds in yonder east:
Night's candles are burnt out, and jocund day
Stands tiptoe on the misty mountain tops.
I must be gone and live, or stay and die.

JULIET

Yon light is not day-light, I know it, I:
It is some meteor that the sun exhales,
To be to thee this night a torch-bearer,
And light thee on thy way to Mantua:
Therefore stay yet; thou need'st not to be gone.

ROMEO

Let me be ta'en, let me be put to death;
I am content, so thou wilt have it so.
I'll say yon grey is not the morning's eye,
'Tis but the pale reflex of Cynthia's brow;
Nor that is not the lark, whose notes do beat
The vaulty heaven so high above our heads:
I have more care to stay than will to go:
Come, death, and welcome! Juliet wills it so.

How is't, my soul? let's talk; it is not day.
JULIET
It is, it is: hie hence, be gone, away!
It is the lark that sings so out of tune,
Straining harsh discords and unpleasing sharps.
Some say the lark makes sweet division;
This doth not so, for she divideth us:
Some say the lark and loathed toad change eyes,
O, now I would they had changed voices too!
Since arm from arm that voice doth us affray,
Hunting thee hence with hunt's-up to the day,
O, now be gone; more light and light it grows.
ROMEO
More light and light; more dark and dark our woes!

Enter Nurse, to the chamber

Nurse
Madam!
JULIET
Nurse?
Nurse
Your lady mother is coming to your chamber:
The day is broke; be wary, look about.

Exit

JULIET
Then, window, let day in, and let life out.
ROMEO
Farewell, farewell! one kiss, and I'll descend.
He goeth down

JULIET
Art thou gone so? love, lord, ay, husband, friend!

I must hear from thee every day in the hour,
For in a minute there are many days:
O, by this count I shall be much in years
Ere I again behold my Romeo!
ROMEO
Farewell!
I will omit no opportunity
That may convey my greetings, love, to thee.
JULIET
O think'st thou we shall ever meet again?
ROMEO
I doubt it not; and all these woes shall serve
For sweet discourses in our time to come.
JULIET
O God, I have an ill-divining soul!
Methinks I see thee, now thou art below,
As one dead in the bottom of a tomb:
Either my eyesight fails, or thou look'st pale.
ROMEO
And trust me, love, in my eye so do you:
Dry sorrow drinks our blood. Adieu, adieu!

Exit

JULIET
O fortune, fortune! all men call thee fickle:
If thou art fickle, what dost thou with him.
That is renown'd for faith? Be fickle, fortune;
For then, I hope, thou wilt not keep him long,
But send him back.
LADY CAPULET
[Within] Ho, daughter! are you up?
JULIET
Who is't that calls? is it my lady mother?
Is she not down so late, or up so early?

What unaccustom'd cause procures her hither?

Enter LADY CAPULET

LADY CAPULET
Why, how now, Juliet!
JULIET
Madam, I am not well.
LADY CAPULET
Evermore weeping for your cousin's death?
What, wilt thou wash him from his grave with tears?
An if thou couldst, thou couldst not make him live;
Therefore, have done: some grief shows much of love;
But much of grief shows still some want of wit.
JULIET
Yet let me weep for such a feeling loss.
LADY CAPULET
So shall you feel the loss, but not the friend
Which you weep for.
JULIET
Feeling so the loss,
Cannot choose but ever weep the friend.
LADY CAPULET
Well, girl, thou weep'st not so much for his death,
As that the villain lives which slaughter'd him.
JULIET
What villain madam?
LADY CAPULET
That same villain, Romeo.
JULIET
[Aside] Villain and he be many miles asunder.--
God Pardon him! I do, with all my heart;
And yet no man like he doth grieve my heart.
LADY CAPULET
That is, because the traitor murderer lives.

JULIET
Ay, madam, from the reach of these my hands:
Would none but I might venge my cousin's death!
LADY CAPULET
We will have vengeance for it, fear thou not:
Then weep no more. I'll send to one in Mantua,
Where that same banish'd runagate doth live,
Shall give him such an unaccustom'd dram,
That he shall soon keep Tybalt company:
And then, I hope, thou wilt be satisfied.
JULIET
Indeed, I never shall be satisfied
With Romeo, till I behold him--dead--
Is my poor heart for a kinsman vex'd.
Madam, if you could find out but a man
To bear a poison, I would temper it;
That Romeo should, upon receipt thereof,
Soon sleep in quiet. O, how my heart abhors
To hear him named, and cannot come to him.
To wreak the love I bore my cousin
Upon his body that slaughter'd him!
LADY CAPULET
Find thou the means, and I'll find such a man.
But now I'll tell thee joyful tidings, girl.
JULIET
And joy comes well in such a needy time:
What are they, I beseech your ladyship?
LADY CAPULET
Well, well, thou hast a careful father, child;
One who, to put thee from thy heaviness,
Hath sorted out a sudden day of joy,
That thou expect'st not nor I look'd not for.
JULIET
Madam, in happy time, what day is that?

LADY CAPULET
Marry, my child, early next Thursday morn,
The gallant, young and noble gentleman,
The County Paris, at Saint Peter's Church,
Shall happily make thee there a joyful bride.
JULIET
Now, by Saint Peter's Church and Peter too,
He shall not make me there a joyful bride.
I wonder at this haste; that I must wed
Ere he, that should be husband, comes to woo.
I pray you, tell my lord and father, madam,
I will not marry yet; and, when I do, I swear,
It shall be Romeo, whom you know I hate,
Rather than Paris. These are news indeed!
LADY CAPULET
Here comes your father; tell him so yourself,
And see how he will take it at your hands.

Enter CAPULET and Nurse

CAPULET
When the sun sets, the air doth drizzle dew;
But for the sunset of my brother's son
It rains downright.
How now! a conduit, girl? what, still in tears?
Evermore showering? In one little body
Thou counterfeit'st a bark, a sea, a wind;
For still thy eyes, which I may call the sea,
Do ebb and flow with tears; the bark thy body is,
Sailing in this salt flood; the winds, thy sighs;
Who, raging with thy tears, and they with them,
Without a sudden calm, will overset
Thy tempest-tossed body. How now, wife!
Have you deliver'd to her our decree?
LADY CAPULET

Ay, sir; but she will none, she gives you thanks.
I would the fool were married to her grave!

CAPULET
Soft! take me with you, take me with you, wife.
How! will she none? doth she not give us thanks?
Is she not proud? doth she not count her blest,
Unworthy as she is, that we have wrought
So worthy a gentleman to be her bridegroom?

JULIET
Not proud, you have; but thankful, that you have:
Proud can I never be of what I hate;
But thankful even for hate, that is meant love.

CAPULET
How now, how now, chop-logic! What is this?
'Proud,' and 'I thank you,' and 'I thank you not;'
And yet 'not proud,' mistress minion, you,
Thank me no thankings, nor, proud me no prouds,
But fettle your fine joints 'gainst Thursday next,
To go with Paris to Saint Peter's Church,
Or I will drag thee on a hurdle thither.
Out, you green-sickness carrion! out, you baggage!
You tallow-face!

LADY CAPULET
Fie, fie! what, are you mad?

JULIET
Good father, I beseech you on my knees,
Hear me with patience but to speak a word.

CAPULET
Hang thee, young baggage! disobedient wretch!
I tell thee what: get thee to church o' Thursday,
Or never after look me in the face:
Speak not, reply not, do not answer me;
My fingers itch. Wife, we scarce thought us blest
That God had lent us but this only child;

But now I see this one is one too much,
And that we have a curse in having her:
Out on her, hilding!
Nurse
God in heaven bless her!
You are to blame, my lord, to rate her so.
CAPULET
And why, my lady wisdom? hold your tongue,
Good prudence; smatter with your gossips, go.
Nurse
I speak no treason.
CAPULET
O, God ye god-den.
Nurse
May not one speak?
CAPULET
Peace, you mumbling fool!
Utter your gravity o'er a gossip's bowl;
For here we need it not.
LADY CAPULET
You are too hot.
CAPULET
God's bread! it makes me mad:
Day, night, hour, tide, time, work, play,
Alone, in company, still my care hath been
To have her match'd: and having now provided
A gentleman of noble parentage,
Of fair demesnes, youthful, and nobly train'd,
Stuff'd, as they say, with honourable parts,
Proportion'd as one's thought would wish a man;
And then to have a wretched puling fool,
A whining mammet, in her fortune's tender,
To answer 'I'll not wed; I cannot love,
I am too young; I pray you, pardon me.'

But, as you will not wed, I'll pardon you:
Graze where you will you shall not house with me:
Look to't, think on't, I do not use to jest.
Thursday is near; lay hand on heart, advise:
An you be mine, I'll give you to my friend;
And you be not, hang, beg, starve, die in
the streets,
For, by my soul, I'll ne'er acknowledge thee,
Nor what is mine shall never do thee good:
Trust to't, bethink you; I'll not be forsworn.

Exit

JULIET
Is there no pity sitting in the clouds,
That sees into the bottom of my grief?
O, sweet my mother, cast me not away!
Delay this marriage for a month, a week;
Or, if you do not, make the bridal bed
In that dim monument where Tybalt lies.
LADY CAPULET
Talk not to me, for I'll not speak a word:
Do as thou wilt, for I have done with thee.

Exit

JULIET
O God!--O nurse, how shall this be prevented?
My husband is on earth, my faith in heaven;
How shall that faith return again to earth,
Unless that husband send it me from heaven
By leaving earth? comfort me, counsel me.
Alack, alack, that heaven should practise stratagems
Upon so soft a subject as myself!
What say'st thou? hast thou not a word of joy?

Some comfort, nurse.

Nurse

Faith, here it is.
Romeo is banish'd; and all the world to nothing,
That he dares ne'er come back to challenge you;
Or, if he do, it needs must be by stealth.
Then, since the case so stands as now it doth,
I think it best you married with the county.
O, he's a lovely gentleman!
Romeo's a dishclout to him: an eagle, madam,
Hath not so green, so quick, so fair an eye
As Paris hath. Beshrew my very heart,
I think you are happy in this second match,
For it excels your first: or if it did not,
Your first is dead; or 'twere as good he were,
As living here and you no use of him.

JULIET

Speakest thou from thy heart?

Nurse

And from my soul too;
Or else beshrew them both.

JULIET

Amen!

Nurse

What?

JULIET

Well, thou hast comforted me marvellous much.
Go in: and tell my lady I am gone,
Having displeased my father, to Laurence' cell,
To make confession and to be absolved.

Nurse

Marry, I will; and this is wisely done.

Exit

JULIET

Ancient damnation! O most wicked fiend!
Is it more sin to wish me thus forsworn,
Or to dispraise my lord with that same tongue
Which she hath praised him with above compare
So many thousand times? Go, counsellor;
Thou and my bosom henceforth shall be twain.
I'll to the friar, to know his remedy:
If all else fail, myself have power to die.

Exit

ACT IV

SCENE I.

Friar Laurence's cell.

Enter FRIAR LAURENCE and PARIS

FRIAR LAURENCE
On Thursday, sir? the time is very short.
PARIS
My father Capulet will have it so;
And I am nothing slow to slack his haste.
FRIAR LAURENCE
You say you do not know the lady's mind:
Uneven is the course, I like it not.
PARIS
Immoderately she weeps for Tybalt's death,
And therefore have I little talk'd of love;
For Venus smiles not in a house of tears.
Now, sir, her father counts it dangerous
That she doth give her sorrow so much sway,
And in his wisdom hastes our marriage,
To stop the inundation of her tears;
Which, too much minded by herself alone,
May be put from her by society:
Now do you know the reason of this haste.
FRIAR LAURENCE
[Aside] I would I knew not why it should be slow'd.
Look, sir, here comes the lady towards my cell.

Enter JULIET

PARIS
Happily met, my lady and my wife!

102

JULIET
That may be, sir, when I may be a wife.
PARIS
That may be must be, love, on Thursday next.
JULIET
What must be shall be.
FRIAR LAURENCE
That's a certain text.
PARIS
Come you to make confession to this father?
JULIET
To answer that, I should confess to you.
PARIS
Do not deny to him that you love me.
JULIET
I will confess to you that I love him.
PARIS
So will ye, I am sure, that you love me.
JULIET
If I do so, it will be of more price,
Being spoke behind your back, than to your face.
PARIS
Poor soul, thy face is much abused with tears.
JULIET
The tears have got small victory by that;
For it was bad enough before their spite.
PARIS
Thou wrong'st it, more than tears, with that report.
JULIET
That is no slander, sir, which is a truth;
And what I spake, I spake it to my face.
PARIS
Thy face is mine, and thou hast slander'd it.
JULIET

It may be so, for it is not mine own.
Are you at leisure, holy father, now;
Or shall I come to you at evening mass?
FRIAR LAURENCE
My leisure serves me, pensive daughter, now.
My lord, we must entreat the time alone.
PARIS
God shield I should disturb devotion!
Juliet, on Thursday early will I rouse ye:
Till then, adieu; and keep this holy kiss.

Exit

JULIET
O shut the door! and when thou hast done so,
Come weep with me; past hope, past cure, past help!
FRIAR LAURENCE
Ah, Juliet, I already know thy grief;
It strains me past the compass of my wits:
I hear thou must, and nothing may prorogue it,
On Thursday next be married to this county.
JULIET
Tell me not, friar, that thou hear'st of this,
Unless thou tell me how I may prevent it:
If, in thy wisdom, thou canst give no help,
Do thou but call my resolution wise,
And with this knife I'll help it presently.
God join'd my heart and Romeo's, thou our hands;
And ere this hand, by thee to Romeo seal'd,
Shall be the label to another deed,
Or my true heart with treacherous revolt
Turn to another, this shall slay them both:
Therefore, out of thy long-experienced time,
Give me some present counsel, or, behold,
'Twixt my extremes and me this bloody knife

Shall play the umpire, arbitrating that
Which the commission of thy years and art
Could to no issue of true honour bring.
Be not so long to speak; I long to die,
If what thou speak'st speak not of remedy.
FRIAR LAURENCE
Hold, daughter: I do spy a kind of hope,
Which craves as desperate an execution.
As that is desperate which we would prevent.
If, rather than to marry County Paris,
Thou hast the strength of will to slay thyself,
Then is it likely thou wilt undertake
A thing like death to chide away this shame,
That copest with death himself to scape from it:
And, if thou darest, I'll give thee remedy.
JULIET
O, bid me leap, rather than marry Paris,
From off the battlements of yonder tower;
Or walk in thievish ways; or bid me lurk
Where serpents are; chain me with roaring bears;
Or shut me nightly in a charnel-house,
O'er-cover'd quite with dead men's rattling bones,
With reeky shanks and yellow chapless skulls;
Or bid me go into a new-made grave
And hide me with a dead man in his shroud;
Things that, to hear them told, have made me tremble;
And I will do it without fear or doubt,
To live an unstain'd wife to my sweet love.
FRIAR LAURENCE
Hold, then; go home, be merry, give consent
To marry Paris: Wednesday is to-morrow:
To-morrow night look that thou lie alone;
Let not thy nurse lie with thee in thy chamber:
Take thou this vial, being then in bed,

And this distilled liquor drink thou off;
When presently through all thy veins shall run
A cold and drowsy humour, for no pulse
Shall keep his native progress, but surcease:
No warmth, no breath, shall testify thou livest;
The roses in thy lips and cheeks shall fade
To paly ashes, thy eyes' windows fall,
Like death, when he shuts up the day of life;
Each part, deprived of supple government,
Shall, stiff and stark and cold, appear like death:
And in this borrow'd likeness of shrunk death
Thou shalt continue two and forty hours,
And then awake as from a pleasant sleep.
Now, when the bridegroom in the morning comes
To rouse thee from thy bed, there art thou dead:
Then, as the manner of our country is,
In thy best robes uncover'd on the bier
Thou shalt be borne to that same ancient vault
Where all the kindred of the Capulets lie.
In the mean time, against thou shalt awake,
Shall Romeo by my letters know our drift,
And hither shall he come: and he and I
Will watch thy waking, and that very night
Shall Romeo bear thee hence to Mantua.
And this shall free thee from this present shame;
If no inconstant toy, nor womanish fear,
Abate thy valour in the acting it.
JULIET
Give me, give me! O, tell not me of fear!
FRIAR LAURENCE
Hold; get you gone, be strong and prosperous
In this resolve: I'll send a friar with speed
To Mantua, with my letters to thy lord.
JULIET

106

Love give me strength! and strength shall help afford.
Farewell, dear father!

Exeunt

SCENE II.

Hall in Capulet's house.

*Enter CAPULET, LADY CAPULET, Nurse, and two
Servingmen*

CAPULET
So many guests invite as here are writ.

Exit First Servant

Sirrah, go hire me twenty cunning cooks.
Second Servant
You shall have none ill, sir; for I'll try if they
can lick their fingers.
CAPULET
How canst thou try them so?
Second Servant
Marry, sir, 'tis an ill cook that cannot lick his
own fingers: therefore he that cannot lick his
fingers goes not with me.
CAPULET
Go, be gone.

Exit Second Servant

We shall be much unfurnished for this time.
What, is my daughter gone to Friar Laurence?
Nurse

Ay, forsooth.
CAPULET
Well, he may chance to do some good on her:
A peevish self-will'd harlotry it is.
Nurse
See where she comes from shrift with merry look.

Enter JULIET

CAPULET
How now, my headstrong! where have you been
gadding?
JULIET
Where I have learn'd me to repent the sin
Of disobedient opposition
To you and your behests, and am enjoin'd
By holy Laurence to fall prostrate here,
And beg your pardon: pardon, I beseech you!
Henceforward I am ever ruled by you.
CAPULET
Send for the county; go tell him of this:
I'll have this knot knit up to-morrow morning.
JULIET
I met the youthful lord at Laurence' cell;
And gave him what becomed love I might,
Not step o'er the bounds of modesty.
CAPULET
Why, I am glad on't; this is well: stand up:
This is as't should be. Let me see the county;
Ay, marry, go, I say, and fetch him hither.
Now, afore God! this reverend holy friar,
Our whole city is much bound to him.
JULIET
Nurse, will you go with me into my closet,
To help me sort such needful ornaments

As you think fit to furnish me to-morrow?
LADY CAPULET
No, not till Thursday; there is time enough.
CAPULET
Go, nurse, go with her: we'll to church to-morrow.

Exeunt JULIET and Nurse

LADY CAPULET
We shall be short in our provision:
'Tis now near night.
CAPULET
Tush, I will stir about,
And all things shall be well, I warrant thee, wife:
Go thou to Juliet, help to deck up her;
I'll not to bed to-night; let me alone;
I'll play the housewife for this once. What, ho!
They are all forth. Well, I will walk myself
To County Paris, to prepare him up
Against to-morrow: my heart is wondrous light,
Since this same wayward girl is so reclaim'd.

Exeunt

SCENE III.

Juliet's chamber.

Enter JULIET and Nurse

JULIET
Ay, those attires are best: but, gentle nurse,
I pray thee, leave me to my self to-night,
For I have need of many orisons
To move the heavens to smile upon my state,
Which, well thou know'st, is cross, and full of sin.

Enter LADY CAPULET

LADY CAPULET
What, are you busy, ho? need you my help?
JULIET
No, madam; we have cull'd such necessaries
As are behoveful for our state to-morrow:
So please you, let me now be left alone,
And let the nurse this night sit up with you;
For, I am sure, you have your hands full all,
In this so sudden business.
LADY CAPULET
Good night:
Get thee to bed, and rest; for thou hast need.

Exeunt LADY CAPULET and Nurse

JULIET
Farewell! God knows when we shall meet again.
I have a faint cold fear thrills through my veins,
That almost freezes up the heat of life:
I'll call them back again to comfort me:
Nurse! What should she do here?
My dismal scene I needs must act alone.
Come, vial.
What if this mixture do not work at all?
Shall I be married then to-morrow morning?
No, no: this shall forbid it: lie thou there.

Laying down her dagger

What if it be a poison, which the friar
Subtly hath minister'd to have me dead,
Lest in this marriage he should be dishonour'd,
Because he married me before to Romeo?

110

I fear it is: and yet, methinks, it should not,
For he hath still been tried a holy man.
How if, when I am laid into the tomb,
I wake before the time that Romeo
Come to redeem me? there's a fearful point!
Shall I not, then, be stifled in the vault,
To whose foul mouth no healthsome air breathes in,
And there die strangled ere my Romeo comes?
Or, if I live, is it not very like,
The horrible conceit of death and night,
Together with the terror of the place,--
As in a vault, an ancient receptacle,
Where, for these many hundred years, the bones
Of all my buried ancestors are packed:
Where bloody Tybalt, yet but green in earth,
Lies festering in his shroud; where, as they say,
At some hours in the night spirits resort;--
Alack, alack, is it not like that I,
So early waking, what with loathsome smells,
And shrieks like mandrakes' torn out of the earth,
That living mortals, hearing them, run mad:--
O, if I wake, shall I not be distraught,
Environed with all these hideous fears?
And madly play with my forefather's joints?
And pluck the mangled Tybalt from his shroud?
And, in this rage, with some great kinsman's bone,
As with a club, dash out my desperate brains?
O, look! methinks I see my cousin's ghost
Seeking out Romeo, that did spit his body
Upon a rapier's point: stay, Tybalt, stay!
Romeo, I come! this do I drink to thee.

She falls upon her bed, within the curtains

SCENE IV.

Hall in Capulet's house.

Enter LADY CAPULET and Nurse

LADY CAPULET

Hold, take these keys, and fetch more spices, nurse.

Nurse

They call for dates and quinces in the pastry.

Enter CAPULET

CAPULET

Come, stir, stir, stir! the second cock hath crow'd,
The curfew-bell hath rung, 'tis three o'clock:
Look to the baked meats, good Angelica:
Spare not for the cost.

Nurse

Go, you cot-quean, go,
Get you to bed; faith, You'll be sick to-morrow
For this night's watching.

CAPULET

No, not a whit: what! I have watch'd ere now
All night for lesser cause, and ne'er been sick.

LADY CAPULET

Ay, you have been a mouse-hunt in your time;
But I will watch you from such watching now.

Exeunt LADY CAPULET and Nurse

CAPULET

A jealous hood, a jealous hood!

Enter three or four Servingmen, with spits, logs, and baskets

Now, fellow,
What's there?

Romeo and Juliet — Act IV

First Servant
Things for the cook, sir; but I know not what.
CAPULET
Make haste, make haste.

Exit First Servant

Sirrah, fetch drier logs:
Call Peter, he will show thee where they are.
Second Servant
I have a head, sir, that will find out logs,
And never trouble Peter for the matter.

Exit

CAPULET
Mass, and well said; a merry whoreson, ha!
Thou shalt be logger-head. Good faith, 'tis day:
The county will be here with music straight,
For so he said he would: I hear him near.

Music within

Nurse! Wife! What, ho! What, nurse, I say!

Re-enter Nurse

Go waken Juliet, go and trim her up;
I'll go and chat with Paris: hie, make haste,
Make haste; the bridegroom he is come already:
Make haste, I say.

Exeunt

113

SCENE V.

Juliet's chamber.

Enter Nurse

Nurse
Mistress! what, mistress! Juliet! fast, I warrant her, she:
Why, lamb! why, lady! fie, you slug-a-bed!
Why, love, I say! madam! sweet-heart! why, bride!
What, not a word? you take your pennyworths now;
Sleep for a week; for the next night, I warrant,
The County Paris hath set up his rest,
That you shall rest but little. God forgive me,
Marry, and amen, how sound is she asleep!
I must needs wake her. Madam, madam, madam!
Ay, let the county take you in your bed;
He'll fright you up, i' faith. Will it not be?

Undraws the curtains

What, dress'd! and in your clothes! and down again!
I must needs wake you; Lady! lady! lady!
Alas, alas! Help, help! my lady's dead!
O, well-a-day, that ever I was born!
Some aqua vitae, ho! My lord! my lady!

Enter LADY CAPULET

LADY CAPULET
What noise is here?
Nurse
O lamentable day!
LADY CAPULET
What is the matter?
Nurse
Look, look! O heavy day!

LADY CAPULET
O me, O me! My child, my only life,
Revive, look up, or I will die with thee!
Help, help! Call help.

Enter CAPULET

CAPULET
For shame, bring Juliet forth; her lord is come.
Nurse
She's dead, deceased, she's dead; alack the day!
LADY CAPULET
Alack the day, she's dead, she's dead, she's dead!
CAPULET
Ha! let me see her: out, alas! she's cold:
Her blood is settled, and her joints are stiff;
Life and these lips have long been separated:
Death lies on her like an untimely frost
Upon the sweetest flower of all the field.
Nurse
O lamentable day!
LADY CAPULET
O woful time!
CAPULET
Death, that hath ta'en her hence to make me wail,
Ties up my tongue, and will not let me speak.

Enter FRIAR LAURENCE and PARIS, with Musicians

FRIAR LAURENCE
Come, is the bride ready to go to church?
CAPULET
Ready to go, but never to return.
O son! the night before thy wedding-day
Hath Death lain with thy wife. There she lies,

Flower as she was, deflowered by him.
Death is my son-in-law, Death is my heir;
My daughter he hath wedded: I will die,
And leave him all; life, living, all is Death's.
PARIS
Have I thought long to see this morning's face,
And doth it give me such a sight as this?
LADY CAPULET
Accursed, unhappy, wretched, hateful day!
Most miserable hour that e'er time saw
In lasting labour of his pilgrimage!
But one, poor one, one poor and loving child,
But one thing to rejoice and solace in,
And cruel death hath catch'd it from my sight!
Nurse
O woe! O woful, woful, woful day!
Most lamentable day, most woful day,
That ever, ever, I did yet behold!
O day! O day! O day! O hateful day!
Never was seen so black a day as this:
O woful day, O woful day!
PARIS
Beguiled, divorced, wronged, spited, slain!
Most detestable death, by thee beguil'd,
By cruel cruel thee quite overthrown!
O love! O life! not life, but love in death!
CAPULET
Despised, distressed, hated, martyr'd, kill'd!
Uncomfortable time, why camest thou now
To murder, murder our solemnity?
O child! O child! my soul, and not my child!
Dead art thou! Alack! my child is dead;
And with my child my joys are buried.
FRIAR LAURENCE

Peace, ho, for shame! confusion's cure lives not
In these confusions. Heaven and yourself
Had part in this fair maid; now heaven hath all,
And all the better is it for the maid:
Your part in her you could not keep from death,
But heaven keeps his part in eternal life.
The most you sought was her promotion;
For 'twas your heaven she should be advanced:
And weep ye now, seeing she is advanced
Above the clouds, as high as heaven itself?
O, in this love, you love your child so ill,
That you run mad, seeing that she is well:
She's not well married that lives married long;
But she's best married that dies married young.
Dry up your tears, and stick your rosemary
On this fair corse; and, as the custom is,
In all her best array bear her to church:
For though fond nature bids us an lament,
Yet nature's tears are reason's merriment.
CAPULET
All things that we ordained festival,
Turn from their office to black funeral;
Our instruments to melancholy bells,
Our wedding cheer to a sad burial feast,
Our solemn hymns to sullen dirges change,
Our bridal flowers serve for a buried corse,
And all things change them to the contrary.
FRIAR LAURENCE
Sir, go you in; and, madam, go with him;
And go, Sir Paris; every one prepare
To follow this fair corse unto her grave:
The heavens do lour upon you for some ill;
Move them no more by crossing their high will.

117

Exeunt CAPULET, LADY CAPULET, PARIS, and FRIAR LAURENCE

First Musician
Faith, we may put up our pipes, and be gone.
Nurse
Honest goodfellows, ah, put up, put up;
For, well you know, this is a pitiful case.

Exit

First Musician
Ay, by my troth, the case may be amended.

Enter PETER

PETER
Musicians, O, musicians, 'Heart's ease, Heart's
ease:' O, an you will have me live, play 'Heart's ease.'
First Musician
Why 'Heart's ease?'
PETER
O, musicians, because my heart itself plays 'My
heart is full of woe:' O, play me some merry dump,
to comfort me.
First Musician
Not a dump we; 'tis no time to play now.
PETER
You will not, then?
First Musician
No.
PETER
I will then give it you soundly.
First Musician
What will you give us?

PETER
No money, on my faith, but the gleek;
I will give you the minstrel.
First Musician
Then I will give you the serving-creature.
PETER
Then will I lay the serving-creature's dagger on
your pate. I will carry no crotchets: I'll re you,
I'll fa you; do you note me?
First Musician
An you re us and fa us, you note us.
Second Musician
Pray you, put up your dagger, and put out your wit.
PETER
Then have at you with my wit! I will dry-beat you
with an iron wit, and put up my iron dagger. Answer
me like men:
'When griping grief the heart doth wound,
And doleful dumps the mind oppress,
Then music with her silver sound'--
why 'silver sound'? why 'music with her silver
sound'? What say you, Simon Catling?
Musician
Marry, sir, because silver hath a sweet sound.
PETER
Pretty! What say you, Hugh Rebeck?
Second Musician
I say 'silver sound,' because musicians sound for silver.
PETER
Pretty too! What say you, James Soundpost?
Third Musician
Faith, I know not what to say.
PETER
O, I cry you mercy; you are the singer: I will say

for you. It is 'music with her silver sound,'
because musicians have no gold for sounding:
'Then music with her silver sound
With speedy help doth lend redress.'

Exit

First Musician
    What a pestilent knave is this same!
Second Musician
    Hang him, Jack! Come, we'll in here; tarry for the
    mourners, and stay dinner.

Exeunt

ACT V

SCENE I.

Mantua. A street.

Enter ROMEO

ROMEO
If I may trust the flattering truth of sleep,
My dreams presage some joyful news at hand:
My bosom's lord sits lightly in his throne;
And all this day an unaccustom'd spirit
Lifts me above the ground with cheerful thoughts.
I dreamt my lady came and found me dead--
Strange dream, that gives a dead man leave
to think!--
And breathed such life with kisses in my lips,
That I revived, and was an emperor.
Ah me! how sweet is love itself possess'd,
When but love's shadows are so rich in joy!

Enter BALTHASAR, booted

News from Verona!--How now, Balthasar!
Dost thou not bring me letters from the friar?
How doth my lady? Is my father well?
How fares my Juliet? that I ask again;
For nothing can be ill, if she be well.
BALTHASAR
Then she is well, and nothing can be ill:
Her body sleeps in Capel's monument,
And her immortal part with angels lives.
I saw her laid low in her kindred's vault,
And presently took post to tell it you:

121

O, pardon me for bringing these ill news,
Since you did leave it for my office, sir.
ROMEO
Is it even so? then I defy you, stars!
Thou know'st my lodging: get me ink and paper,
And hire post-horses; I will hence to-night.
BALTHASAR
I do beseech you, sir, have patience:
Your looks are pale and wild, and do import
Some misadventure.
ROMEO
Tush, thou art deceived:
Leave me, and do the thing I bid thee do.
Hast thou no letters to me from the friar?
BALTHASAR
No, my good lord.
ROMEO
No matter: get thee gone,
And hire those horses; I'll be with thee straight.

Exit BALTHASAR

Well, Juliet, I will lie with thee to-night.
Let's see for means: O mischief, thou art swift
To enter in the thoughts of desperate men!
I do remember an apothecary,--
And hereabouts he dwells,--which late I noted
In tatter'd weeds, with overwhelming brows,
Culling of simples; meagre were his looks,
Sharp misery had worn him to the bones:
And in his needy shop a tortoise hung,
An alligator stuff'd, and other skins
Of ill-shaped fishes; and about his shelves
A beggarly account of empty boxes,
Green earthen pots, bladders and musty seeds,

Romeo and Juliet — Act V

Remnants of packthread and old cakes of roses,
Were thinly scatter'd, to make up a show.
Noting this penury, to myself I said
'An if a man did need a poison now,
Whose sale is present death in Mantua,
Here lives a caitiff wretch would sell it him.'
O, this same thought did but forerun my need;
And this same needy man must sell it me.
As I remember, this should be the house.
Being holiday, the beggar's shop is shut.
What, ho! apothecary!

Enter Apothecary

Apothecary
Who calls so loud?
ROMEO
Come hither, man. I see that thou art poor:
Hold, there is forty ducats: let me have
A dram of poison, such soon-speeding gear
As will disperse itself through all the veins
That the life-weary taker may fall dead
And that the trunk may be discharged of breath
As violently as hasty powder fired
Doth hurry from the fatal cannon's womb.
Apothecary
Such mortal drugs I have; but Mantua's law
Is death to any he that utters them.
ROMEO
Art thou so bare and full of wretchedness,
And fear'st to die? famine is in thy cheeks,
Need and oppression starveth in thine eyes,
Contempt and beggary hangs upon thy back;
The world is not thy friend nor the world's law;
The world affords no law to make thee rich;

Then be not poor, but break it, and take this.
Apothecary
  My poverty, but not my will, consents.
ROMEO
  I pay thy poverty, and not thy will.
Apothecary
  Put this in any liquid thing you will,
  And drink it off; and, if you had the strength
  Of twenty men, it would dispatch you straight.
ROMEO
  There is thy gold, worse poison to men's souls,
  Doing more murders in this loathsome world,
  Than these poor compounds that thou mayst not sell.
  I sell thee poison; thou hast sold me none.
  Farewell: buy food, and get thyself in flesh.
  Come, cordial and not poison, go with me
  To Juliet's grave; for there must I use thee.

Exeunt

SCENE II.

Friar Laurence's cell.

Enter FRIAR JOHN

FRIAR JOHN
  Holy Franciscan friar! brother, ho!

Enter FRIAR LAURENCE

FRIAR LAURENCE
  This same should be the voice of Friar John.
  Welcome from Mantua: what says Romeo?
  Or, if his mind be writ, give me his letter.
FRIAR JOHN

Going to find a bare-foot brother out
One of our order, to associate me,
Here in this city visiting the sick,
And finding him, the searchers of the town,
Suspecting that we both were in a house
Where the infectious pestilence did reign,
Seal'd up the doors, and would not let us forth;
So that my speed to Mantua there was stay'd.
FRIAR LAURENCE
Who bare my letter, then, to Romeo?
FRIAR JOHN
I could not send it,--here it is again,--
Nor get a messenger to bring it thee,
So fearful were they of infection.
FRIAR LAURENCE
Unhappy fortune! by my brotherhood,
The letter was not nice but full of charge
Of dear import, and the neglecting it
May do much danger. Friar John, go hence;
Get me an iron crow, and bring it straight
Unto my cell.
FRIAR JOHN
Brother, I'll go and bring it thee.

Exit

FRIAR LAURENCE
Now must I to the monument alone;
Within three hours will fair Juliet wake:
She will beshrew me much that Romeo
Hath had no notice of these accidents;
But I will write again to Mantua,
And keep her at my cell till Romeo come;
Poor living corse, closed in a dead man's tomb!

Exit

SCENE III.

A churchyard; in it a tomb belonging to the Capulets.

Enter PARIS, and his Page bearing flowers and a torch

PARIS
   Give me thy torch, boy: hence, and stand aloof:
   Yet put it out, for I would not be seen.
   Under yond yew-trees lay thee all along,
   Holding thine ear close to the hollow ground;
   So shall no foot upon the churchyard tread,
   Being loose, unfirm, with digging up of graves,
   But thou shalt hear it: whistle then to me,
   As signal that thou hear'st something approach.
   Give me those flowers. Do as I bid thee, go.
PAGE
   [Aside] I am almost afraid to stand alone
   Here in the churchyard; yet I will adventure.

Retires

PARIS
   Sweet flower, with flowers thy bridal bed I strew,--
   O woe! thy canopy is dust and stones;--
   Which with sweet water nightly I will dew,
   Or, wanting that, with tears distill'd by moans:
   The obsequies that I for thee will keep
   Nightly shall be to strew thy grave and weep.

The Page whistles

   The boy gives warning something doth approach.
   What cursed foot wanders this way to-night,
   To cross my obsequies and true love's rite?

126

Romeo and Juliet — Act V

What with a torch! muffle me, night, awhile.

Retires

Enter ROMEO and BALTHASAR, with a torch, mattock, & c

ROMEO
  Give me that mattock and the wrenching iron.
  Hold, take this letter; early in the morning
  See thou deliver it to my lord and father.
  Give me the light: upon thy life, I charge thee,
  Whate'er thou hear'st or seest, stand all aloof,
  And do not interrupt me in my course.
  Why I descend into this bed of death,
  Is partly to behold my lady's face;
  But chiefly to take thence from her dead finger
  A precious ring, a ring that I must use
  In dear employment: therefore hence, be gone:
  But if thou, jealous, dost return to pry
  In what I further shall intend to do,
  By heaven, I will tear thee joint by joint
  And strew this hungry churchyard with thy limbs:
  The time and my intents are savage-wild,
  More fierce and more inexorable far
  Than empty tigers or the roaring sea.
BALTHASAR
  I will be gone, sir, and not trouble you.
ROMEO
  So shalt thou show me friendship. Take thou that:
  Live, and be prosperous: and farewell, good fellow.
BALTHASAR
  [Aside] For all this same, I'll hide me hereabout:
  His looks I fear, and his intents I doubt.

Retires

ROMEO
Thou detestable maw, thou womb of death,
Gorged with the dearest morsel of the earth,
Thus I enforce thy rotten jaws to open,
And, in despite, I'll cram thee with more food!

Opens the tomb

PARIS
This is that banish'd haughty Montague,
That murder'd my love's cousin, with which grief,
It is supposed, the fair creature died;
And here is come to do some villanous shame
To the dead bodies: I will apprehend him.

Comes forward

Stop thy unhallow'd toil, vile Montague!
Can vengeance be pursued further than death?
Condemned villain, I do apprehend thee:
Obey, and go with me; for thou must die.
ROMEO
I must indeed; and therefore came I hither.
Good gentle youth, tempt not a desperate man;
Fly hence, and leave me: think upon these gone;
Let them affright thee. I beseech thee, youth,
Put not another sin upon my head,
By urging me to fury: O, be gone!
By heaven, I love thee better than myself;
For I come hither arm'd against myself:
Stay not, be gone; live, and hereafter say,
A madman's mercy bade thee run away.
PARIS
I do defy thy conjurations,

And apprehend thee for a felon here.
ROMEO
Wilt thou provoke me? then have at thee, boy!

They fight

PAGE
O Lord, they fight! I will go call the watch.

Exit

PARIS
O, I am slain!

Falls

If thou be merciful,
Open the tomb, lay me with Juliet.

Dies

ROMEO
In faith, I will. Let me peruse this face.
Mercutio's kinsman, noble County Paris!
What said my man, when my betossed soul
Did not attend him as we rode? I think
He told me Paris should have married Juliet:
Said he not so? or did I dream it so?
Or am I mad, hearing him talk of Juliet,
To think it was so? O, give me thy hand,
One writ with me in sour misfortune's book!
I'll bury thee in a triumphant grave;
A grave? O no! a lantern, slaughter'd youth,
For here lies Juliet, and her beauty makes
This vault a feasting presence full of light.
Death, lie thou there, by a dead man interr'd.

Romeo and Juliet — Act V

How oft when men are at the point of death
Have they been merry! which their keepers call
A lightning before death: O, how may I
Call this a lightning? O my love! my wife!
Death, that hath suck'd the honey of thy breath,
Hath had no power yet upon thy beauty:
Thou art not conquer'd; beauty's ensign yet
Is crimson in thy lips and in thy cheeks,
And death's pale flag is not advanced there.
Tybalt, liest thou there in thy bloody sheet?
O, what more favour can I do to thee,
Than with that hand that cut thy youth in twain
To sunder his that was thine enemy?
Forgive me, cousin! Ah, dear Juliet,
Why art thou yet so fair? shall I believe
That unsubstantial death is amorous,
And that the lean abhorred monster keeps
Thee here in dark to be his paramour?
For fear of that, I still will stay with thee;
And never from this palace of dim night
Depart again: here, here will I remain
With worms that are thy chamber-maids; O, here
Will I set up my everlasting rest,
And shake the yoke of inauspicious stars
From this world-wearied flesh. Eyes, look your last!
Arms, take your last embrace! and, lips, O you
The doors of breath, seal with a righteous kiss
A dateless bargain to engrossing death!
Come, bitter conduct, come, unsavoury guide!
Thou desperate pilot, now at once run on
The dashing rocks thy sea-sick weary bark!
Here's to my love!

Drinks

O true apothecary!
Thy drugs are quick. Thus with a kiss I die.

Dies

*Enter, at the other end of the churchyard, FRIAR
LAURENCE, with a lantern, crow, and spade*

FRIAR LAURENCE
  Saint Francis be my speed! how oft to-night
  Have my old feet stumbled at graves! Who's there?
BALTHASAR
  Here's one, a friend, and one that knows you well.
FRIAR LAURENCE
  Bliss be upon you! Tell me, good my friend,
  What torch is yond, that vainly lends his light
  To grubs and eyeless skulls? as I discern,
  It burneth in the Capel's monument.
BALTHASAR
  It doth so, holy sir; and there's my master,
  One that you love.
FRIAR LAURENCE
  Who is it?
BALTHASAR
  Romeo.
FRIAR LAURENCE
  How long hath he been there?
BALTHASAR
  Full half an hour.
FRIAR LAURENCE
  Go with me to the vault.
BALTHASAR

I dare not, sir
My master knows not but I am gone hence;
And fearfully did menace me with death,
If I did stay to look on his intents.
FRIAR LAURENCE
Stay, then; I'll go alone. Fear comes upon me:
O, much I fear some ill unlucky thing.
BALTHASAR
As I did sleep under this yew-tree here,
I dreamt my master and another fought,
And that my master slew him.
FRIAR LAURENCE
Romeo!

Advances

Alack, alack, what blood is this, which stains
The stony entrance of this sepulchre?
What mean these masterless and gory swords
To lie discolour'd by this place of peace?

Enters the tomb

Romeo! O, pale! Who else? what, Paris too?
And steep'd in blood? Ah, what an unkind hour
Is guilty of this lamentable chance!
The lady stirs.

JULIET wakes

JULIET
O comfortable friar! where is my lord?
I do remember well where I should be,
And there I am. Where is my Romeo?

Noise within

Romeo and Juliet — Act V

FRIAR LAURENCE
 I hear some noise. Lady, come from that nest
 Of death, contagion, and unnatural sleep:
 A greater power than we can contradict
 Hath thwarted our intents. Come, come away.
 Thy husband in thy bosom there lies dead;
 And Paris too. Come, I'll dispose of thee
 Among a sisterhood of holy nuns:
 Stay not to question, for the watch is coming;
 Come, go, good Juliet,

Noise again

 I dare no longer stay.
JULIET
 Go, get thee hence, for I will not away.

Exit FRIAR LAURENCE

 What's here? a cup, closed in my true love's hand?
 Poison, I see, hath been his timeless end:
 O churl! drunk all, and left no friendly drop
 To help me after? I will kiss thy lips;
 Haply some poison yet doth hang on them,
 To make die with a restorative.

Kisses him

 Thy lips are warm.
First Watchman
 [Within] Lead, boy: which way?
JULIET
 Yea, noise? then I'll be brief. O happy dagger!

Snatching ROMEO's dagger

 This is thy sheath;

Romeo and Juliet — Act V

Stabs herself

there rust, and let me die.

Falls on ROMEO's body, and dies

Enter Watch, with the Page of PARIS

PAGE
This is the place; there, where the torch doth burn.
First Watchman
The ground is bloody; search about the churchyard:
Go, some of you, whoe'er you find attach.
Pitiful sight! here lies the county slain,
And Juliet bleeding, warm, and newly dead,
Who here hath lain these two days buried.
Go, tell the prince: run to the Capulets:
Raise up the Montagues: some others search:
We see the ground whereon these woes do lie;
But the true ground of all these piteous woes
We cannot without circumstance descry.

Re-enter some of the Watch, with BALTHASAR

Second Watchman
Here's Romeo's man; we found him in the churchyard.
First Watchman
Hold him in safety, till the prince come hither.

Re-enter others of the Watch, with FRIAR LAURENCE

Third Watchman
Here is a friar, that trembles, sighs and weeps:
We took this mattock and this spade from him,
As he was coming from this churchyard side.
First Watchman

A great suspicion: stay the friar too.

Enter the PRINCE and Attendants

PRINCE
    What misadventure is so early up,
    That calls our person from our morning's rest?

Enter CAPULET, LADY CAPULET, and others

CAPULET
    What should it be, that they so shriek abroad?
LADY CAPULET
    The people in the street cry Romeo,
    Some Juliet, and some Paris; and all run,
    With open outcry toward our monument.
PRINCE
    What fear is this which startles in our ears?
First Watchman
    Sovereign, here lies the County Paris slain;
    And Romeo dead; and Juliet, dead before,
    Warm and new kill'd.
PRINCE
    Search, seek, and know how this foul murder comes.
First Watchman
    Here is a friar, and slaughter'd Romeo's man;
    With instruments upon them, fit to open
    These dead men's tombs.
CAPULET
    O heavens! O wife, look how our daughter bleeds!
    This dagger hath mista'en--for, lo, his house
    Is empty on the back of Montague,--
    And it mis-sheathed in my daughter's bosom!
LADY CAPULET
    O me! this sight of death is as a bell,

That warns my old age to a sepulchre.

Enter MONTAGUE and others

PRINCE
Come, Montague; for thou art early up,
To see thy son and heir more early down.
MONTAGUE
Alas, my liege, my wife is dead to-night;
Grief of my son's exile hath stopp'd her breath:
What further woe conspires against mine age?
PRINCE
Look, and thou shalt see.
MONTAGUE
O thou untaught! what manners is in this?
To press before thy father to a grave?
PRINCE
Seal up the mouth of outrage for a while,
Till we can clear these ambiguities,
And know their spring, their head, their
true descent;
And then will I be general of your woes,
And lead you even to death: meantime forbear,
And let mischance be slave to patience.
Bring forth the parties of suspicion.
FRIAR LAURENCE
I am the greatest, able to do least,
Yet most suspected, as the time and place
Doth make against me of this direful murder;
And here I stand, both to impeach and purge
Myself condemned and myself excused.
PRINCE
Then say at once what thou dost know in this.
FRIAR LAURENCE
I will be brief, for my short date of breath

Is not so long as is a tedious tale.
Romeo, there dead, was husband to that Juliet;
And she, there dead, that Romeo's faithful wife:
I married them; and their stol'n marriage-day
Was Tybalt's dooms-day, whose untimely death
Banish'd the new-made bridegroom from the city,
For whom, and not for Tybalt, Juliet pined.
You, to remove that siege of grief from her,
Betroth'd and would have married her perforce
To County Paris: then comes she to me,
And, with wild looks, bid me devise some mean
To rid her from this second marriage,
Or in my cell there would she kill herself.
Then gave I her, so tutor'd by my art,
A sleeping potion; which so took effect
As I intended, for it wrought on her
The form of death: meantime I writ to Romeo,
That he should hither come as this dire night,
To help to take her from her borrow'd grave,
Being the time the potion's force should cease.
But he which bore my letter, Friar John,
Was stay'd by accident, and yesternight
Return'd my letter back. Then all alone
At the prefixed hour of her waking,
Came I to take her from her kindred's vault;
Meaning to keep her closely at my cell,
Till I conveniently could send to Romeo:
But when I came, some minute ere the time
Of her awaking, here untimely lay
The noble Paris and true Romeo dead.
She wakes; and I entreated her come forth,
And bear this work of heaven with patience:
But then a noise did scare me from the tomb;
And she, too desperate, would not go with me,

But, as it seems, did violence on herself.
All this I know; and to the marriage
Her nurse is privy: and, if aught in this
Miscarried by my fault, let my old life
Be sacrificed, some hour before his time,
Unto the rigour of severest law.
PRINCE
We still have known thee for a holy man.
Where's Romeo's man? what can he say in this?
BALTHASAR
I brought my master news of Juliet's death;
And then in post he came from Mantua
To this same place, to this same monument.
This letter he early bid me give his father,
And threatened me with death, going in the vault,
I departed not and left him there.
PRINCE
Give me the letter; I will look on it.
Where is the county's page, that raised the watch?
Sirrah, what made your master in this place?
PAGE
He came with flowers to strew his lady's grave;
And bid me stand aloof, and so I did:
Anon comes one with light to ope the tomb;
And by and by my master drew on him;
And then I ran away to call the watch.
PRINCE
This letter doth make good the friar's words,
Their course of love, the tidings of her death:
And here he writes that he did buy a poison
Of a poor 'pothecary, and therewithal
Came to this vault to die, and lie with Juliet.
Where be these enemies? Capulet! Montague!
See, what a scourge is laid upon your hate,

That heaven finds means to kill your joys with love.
And I for winking at your discords too
Have lost a brace of kinsmen: all are punish'd.

CAPULET

O brother Montague, give me thy hand:
This is my daughter's jointure, for no more
Can I demand.

MONTAGUE

But I can give thee more:
For I will raise her statue in pure gold;
That while Verona by that name is known,
There shall no figure at such rate be set
As that of true and faithful Juliet.

CAPULET

As rich shall Romeo's by his lady's lie;
Poor sacrifices of our enmity!

PRINCE

A glooming peace this morning with it brings;
The sun, for sorrow, will not show his head:
Go hence, to have more talk of these sad things;
Some shall be pardon'd, and some punished:
For never was a story of more woe
Than this of Juliet and her Romeo.

Exeunt

Biography

A Short Life of Edward de Vere, 17th Earl of Oxford

by Dr. Kevin Gilvary, President
The de Vere Society

He was born on 12 April 1550 at Castle
Hedingham, his family's ancestral home. His father, John
de Vere, 16th Earl, was Lord Great Chamberlain and
attended the coronations of both Mary and Elizabeth
Tudor. His mother was Margaret Golding. Edward was 11
when, in 1561, Queen Elizabeth visited Hedingham for
four days of masques, feasting and entertainments. When
his father died in 1562, young Oxford left to become, like
Bertram in *All's Well that Ends Well*, a ward of the Crown
under the guardianship of William Cecil, the Queen's
private secretary (later Lord Burghley, Lord Treasurer).
His mother married Charles Tyrrell and seems to have
passed out of the boy's life. His sister Mary went to live
with her stepfather and the siblings were not reunited for
some years.

According to a curriculum in Cecil's own hand,
Edward de Vere's daily studies included dancing, French,
Latin, writing and drawing, cosmography, penmanship,
riding, shooting, exercise and prayer. Edward de Vere
showed a prodigious talent for scholarship from his early
years, and we may ascribe his lifelong love of learning to
the influence of two of his early tutors. The first was Sir
Thomas Smith who was, perhaps, England's most
respected Greek scholar and the former Cambridge tutor
of Sir William Cecil. It was, no doubt, through Cecil's

influence that Edward de Vere spent some time living in the household of Smith in his early years, during which time he spent about five months at Smith's alma mater, Queens' College, Cambridge. Smith was a scholar of widely varied interests – this was reflected in his 400-volume library, some of which is still extant at Cambridge. De Vere's other tutor was Laurence Nowell, who was not only an accomplished cartographer but was also England's premier scholar of Anglo-Saxon literature – it was Nowell who possessed the only known copy of *Beowulf*.

Another important influence on Edward de Vere's early studies was his maternal uncle Arthur Golding, an officer in the Court of Wards under Cecil, who is credited with the translation of Ovid's *Metamorphoses*, published in 1567, a book widely recognised as having a major influence on 'Shakespeare'.

Following on from his matriculation at Cambridge in November 1558, Edward was awarded an honorary MA by Cambridge during a Royal progress in August 1564, and another degree by Oxford University during a Royal progress in 1566. Edward de Vere then attended Gray's Inn to study law. One notable feature of the Elizabethan Inns of Court was a tradition of mounting dramatic productions and of hosting the various touring companies of players.

In 1570 he served in a military campaign in Scotland under the Earl of Sussex. By 1571, he was reported as a leading luminary of the Court and, for a time, a favourite of Queen Elizabeth. In December 1571 he married Anne Cecil, aged 15, daughter of his guardian. This was a dynastic marriage where all the advantage accrued to Cecil who, ennobled as Baron Burghley, had reduced the social gap between himself and the young Earl.

While Oxford was away on a Grand Tour of Europe, he heard that his daughter Elizabeth Vere had been born in July 1575. On his return in early 1576, he appeared to have been convinced that Elizabeth was not his child; consequently he became estranged from Anne for five years, and exiled himself from Court, taking up residence in the Savoy and concerning himself with literary and musical patronage.

Already, in 1573, *Cardanus Comfort* (the Consolations of Boethius) had been translated from Latin by Thomas Bedingfield and dedicated to Oxford; and published with a preface written by him. In 1576 an anthology, *A Paradise of Daintie Devices*, including several poems by Oxford, was published. These are juvenile works but already show affinities, in both style and thought, with those of the mature Shakespeare.

Oxford's Grand Tour had taken in Paris, Strasbourg, Venice, Genoa, Florence, Palermo and, on his way back through France, Rousillon – the setting for *Love's Labour's Lost*. Oxford spent the best part of a year travelling in Italy in 1576, and becoming involved with moneylenders. He came back to England fluent in Italian and well acquainted with the northern Italian cities, to be satirised by Gabriel Harvey as 'The Italian Earl'. On his way back his ship was attacked by pirates in the English Channel (cf. *Hamlet*). Fourteen of 'Shakespeare's' plays have Italian settings, in which he put his detailed knowledge of the country, beyond pure book knowledge, to good use.

1573 saw the birth of Henry Wriothesley, Earl of Southampton. Although history has not bequeathed to us any evidence of a direct relationship between the two men, in the relatively small world of the royal Court, they must have been acquainted with each other. The poems *Venus and Adonis* (1593) and *The Rape of Lucrece* (1594) were dedicated to Southampton. These were the first works to be published under the name 'Shakespeare' and for the next five years the records show the byline 'Shakespeare' to have been associated exclusively with these two poems. Plays under the name 'Shakespeare' did not appear in print until 1598, the year that Lord Burghley died.

In May 1577 Oxford invested in Frobisher's voyage in the ship *Edward Bonaventure*. Despite its name, the ship's voyage across the Atlantic in search of the North-West Passage lost money; consequently he was forced to sell three estates (cf. Hamlet's words 'I am but mad north-north-west' II.1.). In 1578 he invested in Frobisher's second expedition, which also lost money, forcing further sales of estates.

He was mentioned by Gabriel Harvey in an address to Queen Elizabeth in July 1578, as a prolific private poet and one 'whose countenance shakes spears'. In the same year John Lyly, Oxford's secretary, published *Euphues.The Anatomy of Wit*, followed in 1579 by *Euphues and his England*, dedicated to Oxford. These two books launched the fashion for 'Euphuism', a style characterized by high-flown language, satirized in *Love's Labour's Lost*.

In March 1581 Oxford's mistress, Anne Vavasour, who was one of Queen Elizabeth's Ladies of the Bedchamber, gave birth to a son. The lovers and their son were sent to the Tower by an infuriated Queen but swiftly released (cf. *Measure for Measure*). After his release, Oxford was wounded in a street-fight provoked by Thomas Knyvet, a kinsman of Anne Vavasour; affrays continued in the streets of London between the rival gangs of supporters for over a year (cf.*Romeo and Juliet*).

In December 1581 he resumed living with his long-suffering and devoted wife, and accepted Elizabeth

143

Vere as his child. Tragically, their only son died one day after his birth. Three more daughters followed, of whom Susan and Bridget survived.

In 1584, Robert Greene's *Gwydonius; the Card of Fancy* was dedicated to him, identifying him as a 'pre-eminent writer'. In 1586, when he was 36, he served on the tribunal which condemned Mary, Queen of Scots to execution.

In the same year, the Queen awarded Oxford an unconditional pension of £1,000 a year for life (about £500,000 at today's value). The motive for this uncharacteristic generosity on the part of the Queen remains a mystery – no accounting was required of Oxford. Her successor, King James I, continued to pay the pension. In reply to Sir Robert Cecil's request that Lord Sheffield's pension be increased, the King refused, saying, 'Great Oxford got no more . . .', leaving us to wonder why Great Oxford? His greatness does not seem to have resided in war or any of the known offices of State. Perhaps a clue can be found in a letter to Burghley, written in 1594, in which Edward de Vere seeks his favour in a matter involving what he describes as 'in mine office' and that this office is beholden to the Queen.

In 1589, George Puttenham published *The Arte of English Poesie* and this contains the most telling recognition of Edward de Vere's literary standing amongst his contemporaries: 'And in her Majesties time that now is are sprong up an other crew of Courtly makers Noble men and Gentlemen of her Majesties owne servantes, who have written excellently well as it would appeare if their doings could be found out and made publicke with the rest, of which number is first that noble Gentleman Edward Earle of Oxford.'

In 1588 his wife Anne, daughter of Lord Burghley, died and in extant letters written at this time, it is reported that Burghley is so incapacitated by grief over the death of his favourite daughter that he is incapable of conducting any Privy Council business.

Three years later, in 1591, Oxford married another of the Queen's Maids of Honour, Elizabeth Trentham, with whom he finally became the father of a male heir; Henry de Vere, 18th Earl of Oxford. Although there is evidence of his continued involvement in Court affairs, from the date of this marriage Edward de Vere's life at his new home at King's Place in Hackney is perhaps the most obscure of his entire life.

In 1594, his ship the *Edward Bonaventure* was wrecked in Bermuda (cf. *The Tempest*). In January 1595, Elizabeth Vere married William Stanley, 6th Earl of Derby, another literary earl who maintained his own company of players – many scholars believe that *A Midsummer Night's Dream* was written for these festivities which were attended by the whole royal Court.

On September 7 1598, Francis Meres' *Palladis Tamia* was registered for publication, naming Oxford as the 'best for comedy'. This is a vital document in Shakespearean history because it includes the first mention of 'Shakespeare' as a playwright, attributing twelve plays to him; until then Shakespeare's reputation had rested on the two narrative poems only.

Oxford suffered all his life from financial difficulties, much of which can be traced to the fact that Queen Elizabeth handed out the bulk of his estate to her favourite courtier the Earl of Leicester during Oxford's minority as a royal ward (estates which Oxford found almost impossible to reclaim), and the ruinous debt she placed upon him over his marriage to Anne Cecil. It is, however, notable that his new brother-in-law, the wealthy Staffordshire landowner and Knight of the Shire Francis Trentham, took over the management of Edward de

145

Vere's near-bankrupt estate from 1591 and gradually nursed it back to health so that, when Oxford died, all of his massive debts had been cleared.

On the Queen's death in 1603 Oxford wrote eloquently to Sir Robert Cecil, son and heir of Lord Burghley, of his 'great grief'. He wrote, 'In this common shipwreck, mine is above all the rest, who least regarded, though often comforted, she hath left to try my fortune among the alterations of time and chance'.

Oxford died in Hackney in 1604, cause unknown. Parish records state that he was buried in Hackney Church on July 6, but a family history by his first cousin Percival Golding, states 'Edward de Veer … a man in mind and body absolutely accomplished with honorable endowments … lieth buried at Westminster'. No record of such a burial can now be traced in Westminster Abbey, where there is a Vere family tomb.

The Aftermath of Oxford's life and death

During the winter season 1604-05, six of Shakespeare's plays were presented at Court by command of King James I. This has an air of commemoration. In 1609 the *Sonnets* were published in a pirated edition. The famous dedication describes the author as 'our ever-living', a phrase invariably used only of the dead.

In 1622 Henry Peacham published, in *The Compleat Gentelman*, a list of poets who made Elizabeth's reign a 'golden age'. Unaccountably, he omitted Shakespeare but placed the Earl of Oxford in first place in his list – perhaps he knew them to be the same person. This is unlike Meres who included them both – maybe one reason was because he didn't know Oxford and Shakespeare were the same person.

146

We do not know who instigated publication of the First Folio Edition of the Shakespeare plays in 1623, but there is no mention of any executor or relative of Shakspere of Stratford in connection with it. However, of the two brothers who financed it and to whom it was dedicated, one – Philip Earl of Montgomery – was the husband of Oxford's daughter Susan, while the other – William Earl of Pembroke – had once been a suitor for her sister Bridget. Pembroke was Lord Chamberlain, the supreme authority in the world of theatre, and thus in a position to decide which plays were to be published and which suppressed. We also know that Ben Jonson, who wrote much of the introductory material, was an intimate associate of the de Vere family after Oxford's death. The First Folio was therefore very much a family affair, but the family was not the one in Stratford-on-Avon.

An AfterVerse

For those with yet an interest
In strenuous debate
We've compiled a list of books and films
Your appetite to sate.
From this study clear your mind
Of doubt and all misgiving-
Who from us has long since gone
And who is ever-living.

Selected References & Bibliography
About the Author
Edward de Vere, 17th Earl of Oxford

Books

♦ Anderson, M. (2005). *Shakespeare by Another Name: The Life of Edward de Vere, Earl of Oxford, The Man who was Shakespeare.* New York: Gotham Books. *--A physicist by training with research interest in how evidence supports or negates a theory, Mark Anderson spent ten years investigating Edward de Vere as the author of Shake-speare's works.*

♦Farina, William. (2006). *De Vere as Shakespeare: An Oxfordian Reading of the Canon.* Jefferson, NC. McFarland & Company.

--Each of the plays and poems is individually assessed and explored in its own chapter, using the innumerable connections between the text itself and the life of its author, Edward de Vere.

♦ Looney, J. Thomas (2018). *Shakespeare Identified.* Cary, N.C. Veritas Publicaations.
--First published in 1920 this book began the modern Oxfordian movement. From reading it, Sigmund Freud became convinced and John Galsworthy called it "the best detective story I ever read."

♦ Ogburn, C. (1992). *The Mysterious William Shakespeare.* McLean (Va.): EPM.
--An in depth exploration and must read foundational book on the authorship question.

♦Sobran, Joseph. (1997). *Alias Shakespeare: Solving the Greatest Literary Mystery of All Time.* New York; The Free Press, A Division of Simon & Schuster.
--A concise exploration of the puzzling questions surrounding the authorship controversy with the evidence decisively supporting the case for Edward de Vere, the 17th Earl of Oxford, as the rightful author of the Shakespeare plays and poems.

♦Whittemore, Hank. (2016), *100 Reasons Shake-speare Was the Earl of Oxford.* Somerville MA. Forever Press.
►Also with further discussion and public comment at: *Hank Whittemore's Shakespeare Blog.*
     https://hankwhittemore.com/
--In both the book and online blog cited above, Whittemore presents a concise introduction to the

authorship question that examines 100 different aspects, from biographical and historical records, that point to Edward de Vere as the true writer of the Shake-speare plays and poems.

Websites & Videos

▶ De Vere Society. (2019). The de Vere Society – Dedicated to the proposition that the works of Shakespeare were written by Edward de Vere, 17th Earl of Oxford. [online] Deveresociety.co.uk. Available at: https://deveresociety.co.uk
--A very complete resource with substantial biographical and authorship information and links.

▶ The Oxford Fellowship (2019). Shakespeare Oxford Fellowship | Research and Discussion of the Shakespeare Authorship Question. [online] Shakespeare Oxford Fellowship. Available at: https://shakespeareoxfordfellowship.org/
--A seminal online resource especially focusing on the authorship question.

▶ Waugh, A. (2019). Alexander Waugh. [online] YouTube. Available at: https://www.youtube.com/channel/UCHN7SCKlsa9lPYJmqqQ2uIg/featured/
OR simply search: 'Alexander Waugh'
--Alexander Waugh is a leading authorship scholar who has produced many fascinating video presentations on the authorship question. This link is to his YouTube Channel.

► Columbia Pictures & Centropolis Entertainment. (2011). *Anonymous.* Produced and directed by Roland Emmerich. [DVD]
--This mainstream film is both entertaining and enlightening. It presents a superb dramatization of the character of Edward de Vere, setting out in detail the historical and personal context which made his anonymous authorship necessary.

►Centropolis Entertainment and First Folio Pictures. *Last Will and Testament.* (2012). [DVD]
--A thoughtful and ground-breaking video documentary introduction to the Shakespeare authorship question.

Acknowledgment
Our sincere thanks to
The de Vere Society
and
The Shakespeare Oxford Fellowship
for their inspiration, help and support
in creating this series.

Attributions
--Character list from Wikipedia under
the Creative Commons License 3.0
--Play text from the Moby(tm) editions
in the public domain

Photos
Coat of Arms of Edward de Vere
Source: Wikimedia.org
Author: George Baker / Public domain

The Keep at Castle Hedingham
Source: geograph.org.uk
Author: David Phillips / CC BY-SA 2.0

The de Vere Family Coat of Arms
Source: Wikimedia
Author: Rs-nourse / CC BY-SA 3.0
(https://creativecommons.org/licenses/by-sa/3.0)

View from The Minstrels' Gallery, Hedingham Castle
Source: geograph.org.uk/p/3162585
Photo by: © PAUL FARMER - cc-by-sa/2.0

Cover/Inside: The Welbeck portrait of Edward de Vere (1575).
Artist unknown. National Portrait Gallery, London.

This work has been edited and produced by

Verus Publishing
www.verusbooks.com

V | P

www.ingramcontent.com/pod-product-compliance
Lightning Source LLC
Chambersburg PA
CBHW021154160426
42812CB00082B/3008/J